"I like walking, walking up mountains, in the countryside and through cities — and every now and again I have tried to puzzle out what it is about particular places that I find attractive. The simple answer is that from society I have learned certain fashions: that a classic alpine glaciated peak is 'beautiful', that old thatched cottages are 'picturesque', or that a European cathedral city is 'alive with history'. But how did society come to invent such fashions?"

This wide-ranging book probes the deep-rooted ideas which mould our dealings with the world in which we live. It challenges current views of the environment. It gives a fresh understanding of how we experience the world about us — whether we simply enjoy a day out or are actively concerned in planning or conservation.

"Some years back, I recall going round an exhibition of landscapes by local painters. Walking home, I saw my familiar environment in a totally new and fresh way, for which I was profoundly grateful. If this book does something similar for the reader, then it will have succeeded."

Dr Tony Walter earns his living working part-time for a builders' firm 'at the blunt end of a shovel'. He spends the rest of his time working as a freelance writer. He is a founder member of the Ilkley Group, which explores Christian views of sociology.

To my parents,
for instilling in me an interest in buildings
and a love of landscape.

J A Walter

THE HUMAN HOME

The myth of the sacred environment

A LION PAPERBACK

Copyright © 1982 J. A. Walter

Published by
Lion Publishing
Icknield Way, Tring, Herts, England
ISBN 0 85648 394 X
Albatross Books
PO Box 320, Sutherland, NSW 2232, Australia
ISBN 0 86760 343 7

First edition 1982

Printed and bound in Great Britain by
©ollins, Glasgow.

Contents

Preface

'The author hopes it will not be thought
impertinent to say something of the motives which
induced him to enter into the following enquiry.
The matters which make the subject of it had
formerly engaged a great deal of his attention. But
he often found himself greatly at a loss; he found
that he could not reduce his notions to any fixed
or consistent principles; and he had remarked,
that others lay under the same difficulties.'

So wrote Edmund Burke in 1757 at the start of his preface to
his treatise, *The Sublime and the Beautiful*, in which he tried to
find the key to beauty in landscape. That I can echo the words
without reserve 200 years later suggests that maybe we have not
come far in understanding our environment, what we like about
it, and how we relate to it.

Though a sociologist by training, I must confess to being as
interested in places as in people. In particular I like walking –
walking up mountains, in the countryside and through cities –
and every now and then I have tried to puzzle out what it is
about particular places that I find attractive. The simple answer
is that from society I have learned certain fashions: that a classic
alpine glaciated peak is 'beautiful', that old thatched cottages
are picturesque, or that a European cathedral city is 'alive with
history'. But this merely shifts the question one stage back: how
did society come to invent such fashions? Why are mountains,
countryside and old towns valued in our culture?

A second personal puzzle. I am avowedly anti-materialist, and relish living on as little as possible for the simplicity it gives to life, yet I am preoccupied with my possessions. In particular I am preoccupied with arranging them so that I and others may feel at home in my flat. I spend hours worrying over where to put this picture, whether to shift that table. So, am I materialistic or not? I got no help in answering this from the fashionable literature on simple lifestyles.

Like Burke, I wanted answers which were intellectually satisfying, and which made consistent sense of as much as possible of my own and other people's experience of their environment.

I wrote this book stimulated by these problems, but I cannot claim to have answered them to my satisfaction. When leaning over a five-bar Somerset gate enjoying the view near my home, I still do not know why I like it. Nevertheless I have found the exercise of exploring what the contemporary environment means to people well worthwhile and even if I have yet to arrive at my destination the journey has been valuable for its own sake.

What made me realize that the present book was possible was completing an earlier study of images of wilderness (yet to be published) in which I looked in some depth at one particular kind of landscape and its meaning today. I then began to wonder how that kind of inquiry could be extended to any environmental experience, and this book is the result.

Specific intellectual debts are many, but three of the most important should be acknowledged. Historian W. G. Hoskins' book *The Making of the English Landscape* first showed me that landscape could be a subject for intellectual inquiry as well as visual delight. I was then much encouraged by Chinese American geographer Yi-Fu Tuan's book *Topophilia* to think that it was well worth trying to bring a range of disciplines and experiences to bear on the issue. But it was not until I had read Jacques Ellul's theological book *The Meaning of the City* that I could see how actually to go about the task. I had borrowed Ellul's approach in my book *A Long Way From Home*, in which I explored critically how together people construct for themselves a society, a social environment, in which they can feel at home. I then realized that one could use the same approach to explore critically how people construct and construe a *physical* environment in which they feel at home, and this book more or less wrote itself from then on.

My thanks to Wraxall Builders for providing creative manual toil for two days a week which has kept me alive, happy and sane while working on the book – and provided the not irrelevant experience of actually helping create a part of the built environment. Though I cannot claim that life at the blunt end of a shovel necessarily sharpens one's critical faculties, it does provide them with most refreshing rest.

Constructive criticism has come from Lion Publishing, Peter Clegg, Howard Davis, Janice Russell, Derry Watkins, and Keith White. Many thanks also to Wendy Bleathman for proficient typing.

Some years back, I recall going round an exhibition of landscapes by local painters in the art gallery of the town where I then lived. Walking home, I saw my familiar environment in a totally new and fresh way, for which I was profoundly grateful. If this book does something similar for the reader, then it will have succeeded.

Bath, August 1981

Chapter One

INTRODUCTION: AN ENCHANTED WORLD?

'For almost a thousand years the chief creative
force in western civilisation was Christianity.
Then, in about the year 1725, it suddenly declined
and in intellectual society practically disappeared.
Of course, it left a vacuum. People couldn't get on
without a belief in something outside themselves,
and during the next hundred years they concocted
a new belief which, *however irrational it may seem
to us*, has added a great deal to our civilisation: a
belief in the divinity of nature.'

In this passage from his book *Civilisation*, Kenneth Clark is
describing the romantic movement that dominated much of the
philosophy, poetry and painting of the late eighteenth and nineteenth centuries. But I have underlined one phrase, not for what
it says about the romantics of two hundred years ago, but for
what it says about us. Clark is reiterating a widespread belief:
whereas Wordsworth and Blake and company were irrational
enough to believe in the divinity of the natural world, we, by
contrast, are much more sophisticated and rational, much more
down to earth and scientific in our dealings with our physical
environment. *We* call a spade a spade, a mountain a mountain,
and a field a field – no more and no less. Humankind has 'come
of age' in its thinking, especially its thinking about religion;
technological society is, for better or for worse, entirely pragmatic and practical in its dealings with the environment. This is

a claim shared by economists and ecologists, industrialists and environmentalists.

I wonder if they are right, though. And in this book I want to say why.

It seems to me that we continue to experience our physical surroundings in all kinds of ways that are by no means rational or scientific. We imbue our surroundings with meanings that are ultimately still religious: they reflect and attempt to resolve some of our deepest human concerns.

This is true not only of how we view what Wordsworth called 'nature' – daffodils, mountain streams, clouds and so on – but also of all aspects of our environment, the man-made as well as the natural. From the modern city to the interiors of family homes, from urban slums to stately homes, from the weather and the sky above us to our very own bodies – all is seen in relation to our deepest concerns. Moreover, this way of looking at things is institutionalized: for example, in planning legislation, in the creation of national parks, in the ecology movements, in contemporary philosophies about what is 'natural'. It is also true of the way we embody our ideals and values in bricks and mortar.

Put it another way. The 1960s and 70s saw a spate of writing about the environment, involving several disciplines. There have been ecological views of the environment, geological views and geographical views; the views of politicians and planners, of philosophers and psychologists, of artists, architectural historians, developers, conservationists and preservationists. I want to look at the environment through a different lens, the sociology of religion. I want to look at the environment the way a sociologist looks at religion.

Of course, it is a commonplace that certain national shrines are revered in an almost religious way: Westminster Abbey or Shakespeare's birthplace, Wembley football stadium or Lord's cricket ground, Arlington Cemetery or the Grand Canyon. The existence of a few sacred places such as these in an otherwise secular, technocratic, bureaucratic world is commonly acknowledged. But this is not what I am saying. I claim much more, that it is the norm rather than the exception to perceive and deal with the environment in a religious way.

In this, we are perhaps not so different from 'primitive' tribes. Anthropologists have observed how such tribes live in a world of myths, in which religion, culture and the physical environment are all of a piece. Such tribes communally invent and inhabit an ordered image of the universe, a 'cosmos' that unites all aspects of existence (which we separate into 'God', 'man' and 'nature'), so that it is impossible for the anthropologist to study their environmental perception separately from their culture and from their religion. (It is worth mentioning here why I include the human body in a book on landscape. The way we think of and decorate our bodies is part of the human enterprise of imposing order on the physical world and enabling ourselves to feel at home in it. It is significant that our term for the art of beautifying the body, 'cosmetics', derives from the Greek 'cosmos'. Cosmetics has to do with ordering the universe and our place in it.)

In a much quoted article, *The Historical Roots of our Ecologic Crisis* (1967), Lynn White Jr recalls the long established historical fact that the primitive animistic view of the world in which the physical environment was peopled by spirits, gods and demons was dramatically challenged by Judaism and Christianity. These two religions 'disenchanted' the world: the forests were no longer enchanted by the presence of the spirits, and the fields no longer subject to fertility gods. Disenchantment does not mean disillusion, but 'matter-of-factness'. The earth is worthy of our aesthetic appreciation and scientific investigation, but not our worship. Judaism and Christianity asserted a radical break between the divine (the Creator) and the material (Creation). White is quite correct in this part of his argument. But he greatly over-estimates the extent to which this disenchantment has been complete and permanent.[1] As Jesus himself once said, sweep one spirit out of a house and leave it empty, and seven more will soon come in to fill it.

White's article sparked off a debate about the past, present and potential future effect of religion on the way human beings deal with their environment. The debate, like all the major environmental debates of the late 60s and early 70s, had to do with drastic abuses of the environment: pollution, overpopulation, and so on. Subsequent interest in the environment has extended well beyond these major issues, but the debate over the role of religion has not kept up with this wider interest. I hope to remedy this.

There have been many broad-ranging polemics on the environment, and many detailed descriptive studies by academics. This book is neither. It aims to bring together the work of the academics into a broad understanding of how human beings today relate to their physical surroundings. But be assured it is not an arid accumulation of facts, for it is held together – as any book must be – within the framework of my own commitments and beliefs. The book is primarily descriptive, for before we can begin to ask how people *should* relate to their environment, we must understand how they *do* relate to it. The book ends with questions; are the present processes of environmental perception inevitable? Should we rejoice or grieve over them? Should we attempt to change them? Should we see God in nature, enchantment in the forests, ultimate meaning in the material, or should we not? How we answer that central question will crucially affect the environment which, for better or for worse, will be the human home in the coming decades.

Chapter Two

THE RELIGION OF NATURE

'Every walk in the woods is a religious rite . . . If
we do not go to church as much as did our
fathers, we go to the woods much more, and . . .
we now use the word nature very much as our
fathers used the word God.'
The American nature writer, John Burroughs, 1912

The dominant faith of Western civilization for the past 250 years
has been faith in Man.

Unfortunately, this faith has not proved so well placed as its
early proponents, French philosophers such as Voltaire, had
confidently hoped. The first large-scale attempt to put this faith
into practice was the French Revolution, an event whose bar-
barities worried supporters and critics alike. One reaction to this
manifest disappointment in the goodness of man was to turn to
the worship of nature. From medieval times onwards, existence
had been conceived of as three separate entities: God, Man,
and Nature. Once God had been de-throned by the
eighteenth-century Enlightenment and Man had quickly blotted
his copybook in the French Revolution, the third of the trio –
Nature – became a prime candidate for pre-eminence.

Wordsworth's experience is illuminating. Having enthusiastically joined in the French Revolution, he became disillusioned,
and it was out of this disillusion that his reverence for nature
emerged. For him and his fellow romantics, the nature that they
eulogized was not *beautiful* scenes such as the pleasantly composed parklands created by eighteenth-century aristocrats or the

newly enclosed fields of rural England. Such scenes showed the hand of mankind, the improver of nature. No, painters such as Turner were fascinated by wild, untamed nature: the Alpine avalanche threatening to engulf the weary party of travellers; the storm at sea towering over the tiny sailing ship; untouchable natural phenomena such as rainbows and lightning; anything dramatic going on in that place most resilient to human intervention, the sky. Such scenes were what Edmund Burke in his influential and much reprinted *Philosophical Enquiry into the Origin of our Ideas of the Sublime and Beautiful* termed the Sublime, a surer basis for aesthetics than insipid Beauty. For the romantics, nature was totally other than Man, and as untouchable and awesome as God.

The horrors of the industrial revolution in the nineteenth century brought home even more widely than had the French Revolution the fact that something had gone awry with the doctrines of Man and Progress. And so the romantic reverence for nature found acceptance in many quarters throughout the century. Nevertheless, the faith in Man continued and, despite two World Wars, Stalinism, the bomb, Cambodia and Vietnam, it is still flourishing today. One writer, for example, optimistically proposed in 1975 (shortly after the oil crises, Watergate and Vietnam!) that 'It is within ourselves, and within our friends, that many now seek their solutions in what amounts to a religious renewal of faith in people and their imagination'.[1]

It seems that the historian of science Thomas Kuhn[2] was correct when he claimed that basic beliefs common to a community require an astonishing amount of contrary evidence before they are questioned by those who hold them. When the contrary evidence becomes indisputable, a revolution in how people see the world may occur relatively suddenly. It is exactly this that has been happening in the last decade or two. The optimism concerning rationalism and economic growth which had prevailed in the 1950s and early 60s has been challenged by a whole range of critics and dissidents. Some have advocated the line of 'small is beautiful' and 'no-growth', some LSD and Zen Buddhism, some 'mystical immersion in the all'. These are all alternatives to the rational scientific investigation of the particular.

Political ecology

Among these critics, I want to look at those who derive political programmes and moral lessons from the scientific discipline of ecology. In particular I want to look at their view of nature.

Of course, there are substantial differences between contemporary ecologists and late eighteenth-century nature lovers. Crucially, Darwin stands between them. After Darwin, it became difficult to separate man and nature, and much of the message of ecology is that human beings should recognize that they are a part of nature and cannot flout its laws with impunity. As one introductory text says, it is 'essential that we examine ourselves from an ecological point of view and try to place ourselves in a framework which is part of nature'.[3] Nature has become our moral instructor.

Phrases such as 'nature teaches us that . . .' and 'nature tells us that . . .' were common from the mid-nineteenth century onwards, in the wake of the vast accumulation of knowledge about evolutionary processes. Quite *what* nature taught varied wildly, from mutual co-operation to inevitable and bitter competition, and the same variety of lessons are still trotted out to this day. The lessons taught are explicitly moral and political. Ian McHarg, in his book *Design with Nature*, written in 1969, advocates a philosophy of ecological planning in which he stresses that man is not the creator of his own values but must bow to values set by nature. If nature is the very source of values, then clearly it has a rather more exalted role than that of a mere schoolteacher.

Hollywood actor Robert Redford is among the many who are deeply into things natural. He lives on a ranch 8,000 feet 2,400 m up in the mountains of Utah, he loves the desert, and deeply admires the Indians for their respect for nature. He says:

'Nature is right – I believe in the rightness of
nature in every sense, in its wisdom and in the
biological, physical laws of nature being stronger

than ours . . . I think we're a product of nature
and, therefore, don't know more than nature
does.'

Remarkably similar to Wordsworth:

'One impulse from a vernal wood
May teach you more of man,
Of moral evil and of good,
Than all the sages can.'

Coming from a poet, this perhaps may be accepted as poetic
licence, but political ecologists and their followers such as Redford claim to base their views on science. This involves a reversion to 'natural theology', the philosophical view that an 'ought'
can be derived from an 'is'.[4] This is curious, for modern science
is supposed to be based on a strict separation of 'ought' statements from 'is' statements. Political ecology starts from modern
science, but soon moves onto something much more akin to the
medieval theology of Thomas Aquinas, the view that the ultimate truths of existence may be deduced at least partly from
observation of the natural world. I am not necessarily critical of
such a shift; but I do want to point out that this kind of thinking
has as much to do with religion as with science.

This has not been lost on several commentators. Kenneth
Erickson[5] has suggested that the appeal of modern ecological
thinking is that it provides two ingredients that had been missing
in the traditional romantic religion of nature: it provides a sense
of mission and the hope of salvation. The political ecologist's
message of impending doom which awaits us unless we learn the
moral lessons of ecology makes him into a modern missionary,
offering salvation from a future as bleak as any hell-fire-and-
damnation preached of old. The persuasive techniques of the
ecological preachers may be compared to that of old-time
revivalists.

Modern ecology stresses not the Darwinian nature of bitter
struggle for survival, but nature as a stable, harmonious, self-
regulating system. But this benign system is likely to be vengeful

if we sin against it, and this is the basic message of ecological revivalism; we must repent of our ways. Apocalyptic titles such as *The Doomsday Book* and *A Blueprint for Survival* have been best-sellers. Two interesting comparisons may be made here: not only does this reflect the *style* of revivalist preachers, it also reflects their Old Testament theology of a good, benign God who meets out stern justice if we sin against his ways. It also reflects Wordsworth again:

'If having walk'd with Nature
And offered, as far as frailty would allow,
My heart a daily sacrifice to truth
I now affirm of Nature and of Truth
  That their Divinity
Revolts offended at the ways of men.'

One of the *Blueprint* authors, Michael Allaby, uses an even stronger metaphor, elevating the doom-monger from revivalist to demi-god. Ecologists claim to reject the usual technocratic way of controlling, mastering or manipulating nature for human ends. Nevertheless they still share the conventional modern scientific assumption that knowledge is power, that once we understand the laws of nature we will be able to exercise control over our place on this planet. Allaby warns:

'On the philosophical plane, the ecologist who
seeks to manipulate subtly and benignly, while
remaining hidden, may be seeking for himself a
god-like role in the mighty pageant of the general
system.'[6]

Revivalists they may have been in the early 70s, but what they aim at now is to be the high priests of an 'ecocracy', a society run along ecological lines under the benign guidance of the guardians of ecological knowledge. This certainly seemed to have been the intention of the authors of *A Blueprint for Survival* in 1972: 'Basic precepts of ecology, such as the inter-relatedness of all things and the far-reaching effects of ecological processes and their disruption should influence community decision making.' This political philosophy underlies Britain's Ecology Party today.

Now it may be that some of the more extreme views, and certainly the extreme style, of the early 70s have been moderated. But my point is that seeing nature as the bearer of moral values certainly did not die out with nineteenth-century romanticism. One balanced reviewer of the environmental movement of the early 70s has described its hallmark as 'the sense of wonder, reverence and moral obligation' in the presence of nature.[7]

There is an important sense in which this reverence for nature is even more religious than the animism of many so-called 'primitive' peoples. Tribesmen who venerate a sacred mountain do so not because it is a mountain, but because it is sacred; the mountain speaks of something beyond itself, and they know perfectly well that in itself it is no more than a mountain.[8] Likewise in the view of medieval natural theology, nature pointed to God but was not itself God. However, for modern worshippers of nature from the romantics onwards, the sacredness lies in the mountain itself, and for contemporary ecologists it lies in the whole natural system. For the traditionalist, the sacred is worshipped through nature; for the modern, nature itself is worshipped. In this sense, the modern is less sophisticated than the 'primitive'.

Nature's temples

Those who think explicitly in an ecological way, though vocal, are a small minority, in Britain at any rate. But the worship of nature does not depend on an ecological awareness; it is considerably more widespread than is ecology. For the rest of this chapter, I want to examine three particular 'temples', three places of worship in the religion of nature: the wilderness, the countryside and the human body.

That particular aspects of the natural world should take on religious significance is perhaps as old as mankind itself. The sky, for instance, has often been full of symbolic meaning. Being the source of thunder, lightning and hail it can destroy crops and habitations; the source of sun and rain, it provides life and growth. It is hardly surprising that it features strongly in many religions. But its most significant aspect (at least, prior to aviation) has been its total *otherness*. Human beings can till the ground, dig and mine underground, sail the seas and swim in the river, and they have done so since the beginning of recorded history. But one thing they cannot do is fly. The sky cannot be tamed or grasped, and air is much less tangible and comprehensible than solids and liquids. The sky is wholly other than man, and according to the classic formulation which Rudolf Otto made in his book *The Idea of the Holy* this total otherness is the chief characteristic of God. So it is wholly appropriate that in many religions, God should be conceived of as dwelling in the sky, and that heaven should be seen as being up there.[9]

In the 1960s it became fashionable in progressive theological circles to poke fun at the idea of God being 'up there'. In fact this was really quite an appropriate symbol, and ironically the same generation which disenchanted the sky deified something very similar, the wilderness.

The American wilderness

By wilderness I mean those wild places uninhabited by human beings – high mountains, deserts, deep jungles and so on. Contemporary people seem to be fascinated with such places. Their images recur in movies, television documentaries, tourist brochures, calendar pictures, shortbread tins and cigarette advertisements, and have become an accepted part of modern western culture. Preservationists are as keen to preserve the wilderness as they are historical monuments.

What such wild places have in common is their total otherness from the human world. That is what leads people like American conservationist Edward Abbey to make statements as extraordinary as:

'we have agreed not to drive our automobiles into
cathedrals, concert halls, art museums, legislative
assemblies, private bedrooms, or other sanctums
of our culture. We should treat our National Parks

with the same deference, for they, too, are holy
places . . . We are finally learning that the forests
and the mountains and the desert canyons are
holier than our churches.'[10]

Erickson[11] is surely right when he terms the American wilderness
'the sacred shrine of the religion of nature'.

Wilderness, by definition, is where human beings are not, or
at least where they do not live. So wilderness is the supreme
manifestation of nature-without-man, nature in her purity un-
defiled by profane mankind. It attracts those who are worn out
by everyday life. Like Sunday worship for the Christian, a so-
journ in the wilderness is believed to provide contact with the
divine, and restore the soul. It may provide a new and radical
perspective on the banality of everyday existence, or at least
restore one enough to go back to the tread-mill on Monday
morning.

This contrast with the tedium and offence of the everyday
human world was certainly what attracted the wilderness' most
prestigious sponsor in the nineteenth century, Queen Victoria.
She records in her diary the first day at her newly-completed
Balmoral Castle in the Scottish Highlands:

'It was so calm and so solitary, it did one good as
one gazed around, and the pure mountain air was
so refreshing. All seemed to breathe freedom and
peace, and to make one forget the world and its
sad turmoils.'

This scene of blissful purity is still highly valued. An official
tourist brochure for the Balmoral area written in the early 1970s
virtually echoes Victoria's words:

'. . . everywhere all the time the pure, sweet
Highland air, mountains, space, peace and for
those who wish it solitude.'

This reverence for the wilderness is especially potent in the

USA. Americans writing about the wilderness are much stronger in their language than Victoria or her tourist board descendents. The following quotes are from a book edited by David Brower, crusading leader of the influential conservation organization, The Sierra Club, and later leader of Friends of the Earth:

'Wilderness is fairly close to the best place of all in which to find a draft of fresh air, in which to take stock, in which to find yourself, discover the *you* that so many distractions have kept you away from so long that the life you lead is not your own.'

'Some people will be able to walk in wilderness and most of them will be the better for it. Some may wish to but never make it. Some may not think they care to at all, nor expect their sons to care. But wilderness must be there, or the world's a cage.'

'It is this civilization, this culture, this way of living that will be sacrificed if our wilderness is lost. What sacrifice!'[12]

While for Robert Marshall in a much-quoted article:

'In a civilization which requires most lives to be passed amid inordinate dissonance, pressure and intrusion, the chance of retiring now and then to the quietude and privacy of a sylvan haunt becomes for some people a psychic necessity. It is only the possibility of convalescing in the wilderness which saves them from being destroyed by the terrible neural tension of modern existence.'[13]

This desire for temporary escape from the brash world may help explain the current popularity of the American wilderness, but its historical origins do not display the same weariness with ordinary life and ordinary landscapes. When the first English and Dutch settlers arrived in America in the early seventeenth century they had half hoped to find a garden paradise awaiting them. They wanted America to fulfil a dream that had captivated the European imagination since the Latin poet Virgil, a dream of a golden land with fruit dripping from the trees; a land which would end the hard toil of winning a living from the soil. This image was soon to be idealized in the fashionable paintings of the Italian Claude Lorrain. What the settlers found was largely an inhospitable wilderness, with savage winters.[14]

This tension between the hope of a pastoral paradise and the realities of taming an inhospitable wilderness has continued to this day. But after Independence a decisive cultural innovation came about in response to a new need. America needed an independent identity; 'Americans sought something uniquely "American", yet valuable enough to transform embarrassed provincials into proud and confident citizens.'[15] So, through the nineteenth century, some American artists and writers abandoned trying to portray their land as a long-settled and productive landscape – the dominant European style of landscape painting since the seventeenth century – and began to embrace the romantic image of the wilderness. If there was one dramatic landscape that only America had, it was the wilderness, the vast empty spaces of the West. Here at last was something uniquely American. No European nation could match it. America might not have a history, but at least it had a geography.

This felt lack of history did not show itself immediately after Independence. At first Americans prided themselves on looking to the future, unlike a Europe which dragged on with the millstone of history around its neck. But the Civil War produced a crisis of confidence; then came the Centennial which fostered a backward look; then the new waves of immigrants from all around the world, and America began to be concerned about its cultural identity.[16] In this context the world's first national park, Yellowstone, was founded in the 1870s, and a whole spate of 'wilderness novels' and nature writing became best-sellers around the turn of the century. Nature had become almost the official religion of the United States; it was certainly the religion of popular writer John Burroughs in 1912:

'Every walk in the woods is a religious rite . . . If
we do not go to church as much as did our
fathers, we go to the woods much more, and . . .
we now use the word nature very much as our
fathers used the word God.'

America has rejected the European ideal of the Claude's pastoral landscape and has taken for its own the romantic ideal which began with Wordsworth. The worship of nature is nowhere so alive today as in America, and the prime object of its believers' affections is the American wilderness.

Scarcity and sacredness

This image of the wilderness, though, is somewhat precarious. Just as the ecological image of a benign, stable, harmonious Mother Nature is threatened by the Darwinian spectre of a ruthless Nature red in tooth and claw, so the romantic image of the wilderness has to come to terms with the fact that most wild places are rather unpleasant. The Canadian tundra is plagued with midges during the short summer, most pristine forests have a virtually impenetrable undergrowth, swamps are decidedly unhealthy, and many mountains are semi-arid deserts of scree while few are virgin-white peaks rising out of pleasant meadows.

Not only are such places unpleasant, they are also dangerous. In the event of an accident, help may be so far away as to be useless; it is not insignificant that one of the few major air accidents to have no survivors at all happened when a New Zealand tourist plane plunged into Mount Erebus in that biggest wilderness of all – Antarctica. The transition from mystic contemplation to extinction can be devastatingly quick in the wilderness, perhaps nowhere better expressed than in Herman Melville's *Moby Dick* (in which the ocean represents utter wildness and vastness).

Ishmael is in a transcendental reverie while on look-out up the mast:

'But while this sleep, this dream is on ye, move
your feet or hand an inch; slip your hold at all;
and your identity comes back in horror. Over
Descartian vortices you hover. And perhaps, at
mid-day, in the fairest weather, with one half-
throttled shriek you drop through that transparent
air into the summer sea, no more to rise for ever.
Heed it well, ye Pantheists!'

This realism characterizes all who actually venture into the really
wild places, rather than those who just dip a toe in and then
proceed to write mystic poetry. Ask any professional sailor or
astronaut.

Not only is the wilderness usually uncomfortable and dangerous, it is also often ugly. Most deserts are not perfect wind-
blown dunes glistening pure gold or white in the sun; they are
semi-scrub, flat as a pancake, roamed perhaps by half-starved
cattle and acting as a dump for technological refuse such as old
motor cars and abandoned tanks which do not rust or decay in
the dry, pure air. Left to the devices of nature, a Newfoundland
forest may consist of fungus-attacked stunted dwarfs, in contrast
to the healthy tall conifers of a managed plantation.

The problem with actual wild places, then, is not just that
they are physically uncomfortable and dangerous, but that they
also challenge the romantic notion of the purity and beauty of
the Great Goddess Nature. For this notion to stay intact, the
illusion must somehow be fostered that wilderness is pretty and
safe.

In American national parks it is not desired that visitors
should discover the true nature of wild places – dangerous and
uncomfortable. The one consideration for which park managers
are prepared to modify the pristine nature in their parks is the
safety and comfort of the visitors: it is vital that visitors *enjoy*
their time there. As the official brochure for the American
national parks says (emphases mine):

'The natural surroundings of the parks are
permitted only such changes as are necessary to

protect and administer them for the *comfort and
convenience* of visitors. Every effort is made to
preserve the natural state of these parks to
provide an opportunity for visitors to *enjoy* them
and learn from them.'

When these protective facilities cannot be provided, as in winter
in some parks, the park is closed:

'Facilities in many of the Northern parks are
snow-bound and closed during the winter.'

Indeed, national parks have been sued by visitors who have
come to harm. They desire contact with nature, but a benign
nature.

So there is a problem, deriving from the juxtaposition of three
geographical facts:

First, contrary to popular belief, there is masses of wilderness
in the world. To a Martian looking through his telescope, Earth
would appear almost entirely a wilderness. Anthony Smith[17] was
amazed when he looked at his atlas to find that:

'Adding the oceans and the land together, just
nine per cent of the planet's surface could be
cultivated and, of that proportion only a third is
being tilled, a mere three per cent of the
196,950,000 square miles that is the Earth's total
surface area. The Martian's stay-at-home
companions would therefore gain the picture of a
wild world, scarcely touched by its inhabitants and
impossible to use for its major part.'

Second, there are lots of pretty places in the world, and lots
of safe places.

Third, there are rather few places that are both wild and
pretty, dominated by nature yet safe for humans; and still fewer
that are readily accessible for the urban masses. No wonder
Queen Victoria loved her Balmoral retreat where for her 'the

scenery is *wild*, and yet *not desolate*', that is to say, natural yet not ugly. No wonder it is generally only the well-to-do who have the time and money to visit, still less to own, such places.

Together, these three facts cause a problem because, though the overt definition of wilderness is that it is wild, natural and unpopulated, the covert definition insists that it also be pretty, safe and accessible. So there has grown up a myth that *wilderness is scarce*, and fast disappearing. Virtually any valued wild place is believed to be 'the last wilderness'. Thus a television documentary declared the Amazon to be 'the last great natural reserve on earth'; a brochure for holidays in Scotland suggests you 'plan your escape to Britain's last wide-open spaces', while another claims Scotland to be 'one of the last great wild areas of Europe'; a television documentary on the Cairngorm Mountains was entitled 'The Last Wilderness'. Well, they can't all be the last wilderness, but each in its turn is believed to be.

This belief in the scarcity of wilderness greatly enhances its sacredness. Something common could hardly be a viable replacement for God; the substitute must surely be rare, yet accessible; of a different order, yet approachable if one goes through the correct preparatory ritual. Without the myth of scarcity, the religion of Nature could hardly continue.

The English countryside
If nature is valued most highly in those wild places where there is little or no sign of human influence, what about the settled countryside that is considerably more accessible to the vast majority of the British (and in particular the English) population? Here we find a complementary myth. If the wilderness myth would have it that wild nature is beautiful, the countryside myth would have us believe that beautiful farmland countryside is natural. Both equate 'natural' with 'beautiful'. One takes what is natural and insists it is beautiful; the other takes what is beautiful and insists it is natural.

The beautiful English countryside is actually the product of about 1,500 years of mixing Anglo-Saxon labour with the soil, a process nowhere better described than in W. G. Hoskins' *The Making of the English Landscape*. This tradition is one that the world, currently concerned with environmental degradation, could well learn from. Yet, just now, we English are doing our best to hide from the mind's eye all trace of human labour in the landscape. There is currently a vogue for glossy coffee-table books on the countryside, colourful and comprehensive guide books on English villages for motorists, nature films on the television, and calendars of our English 'heritage'. All these portray the English countryside *not* as a product of human labour, but as something that has magically dropped at our feet from the distant past, a product of nature unsullied by the passage of time. Council houses, combine harvesters, rural poverty, declining services and modern capital-intensive agriculture rarely feature in the texts of these books and *never* in the accompanying photographs. This feeds the townsperson's already well-formed illusions about the naturalness of rural landscapes which are in fact the decidedly human products of generations of loving care.

Because he sees the countryside as a product of nature rather than human effort, the townsperson typically believes that it belongs to everyman. This, not surprisingly, leads to conflict with country people; as one of them complains:

'It is because past and present countryfolk have cared for the countryside, the historic towns and villages, that they are now worth visiting and available for recreation. Our "heritage of the countryside" is the creation of generations of country folk, and is as man-made as Euston Station, the Bull Ring in Birmingham and the spoil heaps of Aberfan. The countryside retains its beauty because it is cared for by the country folk of today, who sacrifice many things to live there, accepting lower incomes, inadequate transport services and a general lack of facilities.'[18]

But the townsperson does not wish to know this. Needing, he thinks, to escape for an afternoon or a week from humankind, he does not want to confront the reality of life in the countryside;

he wants to exist for a moment or two in a landscape he believes to be natural.

Where lie the roots of this illusion? One important source is to be found in a key period of English rural history which is full of contradictions – the agricultural improvements carried out by eighteenth-century landowners, and in particular their invention of landscape gardening. Creating landscapes of enduring beauty with extraordinary imagination and skill, men such as William Kent, Lancelot Brown, Humphrey Repton, and Uvedale Price also sowed the seeds of the modern attitude to the countryside which is such a profound lie. They knew that their aristocratic patrons disdained the sweat and toil which was the lot of their labourers and which created a prosperous landscape. They disdained productive activity engaged in for profit, and while making considerable fortunes out of this kind of activity they wanted to keep it at a distance. So the typical re-organization of a great landed estate of the eighteenth century involved landscaping the view in front of the house as parkland, with deer roaming, a glimpse of water, small clumps of trees, and enough open space to see that this leisured landscape extended for some miles. Whole villages were sometimes demolished if they were in the way of the view, and re-erected out of site. Repton declaimed that 'a ploughed field was no fit sight from a gentleman's elegant mansion'.

The intention was to propagate the illusion that the countryside was a product of nature rather than the landscape gardener, still less the humble labourer and tenant farmer. Brown attempted to conceal his own hand in his re-organized landscapes, and took it as the highest complement if a visitor mistook the view as entirely natural. He would have been delighted, for example, had he lived to read the 1797 guide to Burghley House whose grounds he had landscaped twenty years earlier:

'Though the beauties, with which we are here
struck, are more peculiarly the rural beauties of
Mr Brown, than those of Dame Nature, she seems
to wear them with so simple and unaffected a
grace, that it is not even the man of taste who

can, at a superficial glance, discover the
difference.'

Some critics of Brown, however, thought his almost
savannah-like open parklands looked decidedly contrived, and
advocated what quickly became known as the 'picturesque', a
much more intimate landscape which valued thatched cottages,
donkeys, gnarled trees, paths disappearing into thickets, rough
lanes, and even ruins and grottoes. But one thing they shared
with Brown: they had no taste for the countryside as productive
farmland. And their landscapes were far more obviously contrived than Brown's ever were.

These men, then, were the original proponents of the countryside myth: that beautiful countryside is natural, the work of
nature. And they made it clear that it was legitimate to go to
extraordinary lengths to conceal the human hand behind the
landscape. The carefully-contrived illusion is that only nature
can produce beauty; human beings cannot.

The human body

A third sacred shrine in the religion of nature is the human body
itself. At least, this is true according to that important strand in
modern popular thought that makes a cult of the human body.
In the Hollywood version of this cult, what is revered is not
one's own body, but the ideal body: the ideal female body
(Marilyn Monroe), and the ideal male body (Clint Eastwood).
Our own bodies, of course cannot possibly live up to such
elevated (and statistically abnormal) shapes, and so we conceive
of our own bodies as pale imitations. My body is made in the
image of Eastwood's (though a rather poor image) and yours in
the image of Monroe's (though a poor image, too). Ashamed
of and dissatisfied with our own bodies, we engage in regular
rituals to make them more like the ideal. Dieting, bathing,
applying cosmetics, keeping in shape through yoga or jogging,
applying patent remedies for balding heads or sagging breasts
take up vast amounts of time, effort and money. This guilt-
ridden ritual activity seems particularly prevalent in the USA,[19]
and certainly succeeds in producing healthier-looking and appar-

ently more beautiful members of the human species than the wan specimens we are used to in Britain.

Feelings, along with the body, are usually seen as part of Nature, as opposed to mind, conscience and society which are part of Man. Thus, associated with the ideal male and female body are ideal male and female feelings. Men are supposed to feel aggressive, protective toward their womenfolk, and so on; women have maternal instincts and 'naturally' feel warm and caring. As with the body, the feelings real men and women actually have are judged in terms of these feelings of Universal Man and Universal Woman. Because the ideal feeling, like the ideal body, is deemed 'natural', intense guilt can be felt when actual feelings do not match up to the ideal.

Particularly as a result of the women's movement, there has been a reaction against this belief in the ideal Universal Woman (and to some extent also of Universal Man). Increasing numbers of women are accepting their bodies for what they are, and the Ideal Form is parodied as a statistical abnormality, the very opposite of natural. Likewise, many women are now more concerned with acting on the basis of the feelings they actually have rather than trying to mould their feelings into those of Universal Woman.

So, we are beginning to see a shift from reverence for the ideal body to reverence for *my* body, from reverence for the ideal feeling to reverence for *my* feelings. Though this shift from universal to particular is important, there is a key continuity: what is natural is still thought right. All that has changed is *what* is deemed to be natural: the universal or the particular.

The contemporary celebration of the body and of sexual feeling is typical of any nature religion in which 'natural' equals 'good' (and these religions have existed for several thousands of years). Whatever one's body is naturally inclined toward is believed to be right, for the body is part of Nature. Whenever the human mind, the human conscience or human society (in the form of rules and laws) object to the body's inclinations, this is deemed wrong. This is because mind, conscience and society are all part of Man, an untrustworthy being, while body is part of Nature, which may be trusted.

This kind of ultimately religious thinking lies behind much of the scientific effort to disentangle the influences of the environment (human) from heredity (natural) on human behaviour. Biology is part of nature and is therefore inescapably and morally right; culture is part of society and is most likely misguided. At its most naive, this means that the impulse to jump into bed with anyone is more to be trusted than the conscience which may say otherwise. But the same kind of argument is actually repeated on more intellectually sophisticated occasions. For example, it is commonly assumed that because there is a biological basis to homosexuality, this justifies homosexual behaviour. Or, that if it can be shown that blacks are genetically less intelligent than whites, this justifies putting them into an inferior position in a society in which bright is right. Or, that the wide biological range of sexual characteristics *among* males and *among* females is a good reason for breaking down the rigidly different behaviour patterns that men and women are expected to display.

The dominance of this kind of naturalism is shown in the fact that much more time and energy is expended trying to demonstrate the existence or non-existence of biological differences (between men and women, whites and blacks) than discussing the implications of such differences. It is simply assumed that if biological differences exist, then social differences should follow. Liberals who want homosexuals to be allowed to behave differently from other people make great play of the biological difference between homo- and heterosexuals. Liberals who want women to compete on equal terms with men often play down the biological differences between men and women. They feel that biology should determine culture, because the great god Nature is always right. According to naturalists, the trouble with our repressive society is that culture (a male, heterosexual, white culture) has trampled all over nature. This view is directly comparable with the ecological naturalists who castigate technological society for having trampled all over nature.

At the least honest, what happens is that first the conclusion is chosen, and then a biological or ecological basis is sought for it. This is not so very different from the eighteenth-century gardeners who decided what looked beautiful (on really very arbitary grounds) and then set out to convince the world that this was what nature was like all along. As history shows only too well, we human beings are remarkably persistent in our efforts to co-opt God for our own ends, and we do exactly the same with the god of nature.

Naturalism, though influential and often newsworthy, is not the only current view of the body. There is an important strand of thought which accepts the dichotomy of mind and body, but places mind above body. Like naturalism, this view can be pretty extreme. The most obvious case was the Victorian prudishness that repressed awareness of the body and especially awareness of sexuality. Today there is the extreme idealism of some socio-logists who seem to think that mind (in the form of culture) is everything, and matter (in the form of biology) is nothing.

But there are also more reasoned advocates of the supremacy of mind. C. S. Lewis,[20] for example, clearly distinguished Reason from Nature. For Lewis, Reason is not governed by natural forces. On those occasions when it is – as when I think the way I do because I have a liver complaint or because of a poor upbringing or because of my bourgeois position – then it is right to discount the truth or rationality of my thinking; these natural causes are, strictly, irrational. Reason, for Lewis, was strictly *super*natural; so his whole theology was based on the premise that Reason existed autonomously.

In this respect (though not in many others!) Lewis has fellow travellers in those modern liberals who believe in self-determi-nation, in being in control of their lives. They resent having their fates determined by blind forces over which they have no control. Whereas Lewis and the Victorians saw these blind forces in nature, the moderns see them in society. But both affirm the supremacy of mind.

An increasingly fashionable view of the body/mind relation is 'holism', the belief that they are inextricable. This gives pride of place to neither mind nor body, and relishes the exploration of how each influences the other. But it is a difficult stance to maintain, and frequently relapses into one of the other two modes of thinking.

There is no need to explore these two alternatives to naturalism further here, interesting though that would be. It is enough simply to document how the religion of nature is applied to the human body, and to point out that, as in perceptions of ecology, wild places and the countryside, naturalism is by no means the only current philosophy. But I hope to have mustered enough evidence to show that there are significant cultural and philosophical movements influencing us to perceive and experience the natural environment – from planet Earth down to our own bodies – through essentially religious, though not necessarily Christian, spectacles.

Chapter Three

THE SANCTITY OF THE INDIVIDUAL

'Perspective makes the single eye the centre of the visible world . . . The visible world is arranged for the spectator as the universe was once thought to be arranged for God.'

John Berger

Despite excursions into naturalism, the basic modern belief remains faith in Man. This takes two major forms. First, there is faith in the sacred communities of communism and fascism. Second, and more important for this book, there is faith in the sacred individual who is seen as the ultimate end, whose needs the state and society must serve. This individualism is one of the cardinal beliefs of western civilization, expressed most obviously in human rights, especially the freedom of speech and the freedom to own property, and in such major documents as the American constitution. Individualism is the dominant form of the worship of Man in the West.

Individualism profoundly affects how we perceive our physical surroundings. The historical origins of individualism are deep and complex, but a useful point to start an investigation is the Renaissance. This period saw both a major flourishing of individualism and dramatic changes in the visual arts – painting, sculpture, and architecture. These reveal how artists at least were changing their view of the world in line with the new philosophy of individualism.

The crucial invention was that of perspective. This centred

the world around the individual, and has been described by the critic John Berger as follows:

'The convention of perspective, which is unique to European art and which was first established in the early Renaissance, centres everything on the eye of the beholder. It is like a beam from a lighthouse – only instead of light travelling outwards, appearances travel in. The conventions called those appearances *reality*. Perspective makes the single eye the centre of the visible world . . . The visible world is arranged for the spectator as the universe was once thought to be arranged for God.'[1]

Developments in astronomy in the late Renaissance challenged the notion that the universe revolved around the Earth. But the new art that had by then won a total victory proposed something even more anthropocentric than the old astronomy that Copernicus deposed. The Earth was now no longer the centre of the universe, but the individual most certainly was.

Berger illustrates the change by examining what happened to paintings of Adam and Eve in the Garden of Eden.[2] In the medieval tradition the story was often illustrated scene by scene as in a strip cartoon – a real historical sequence which existed independent of the onlooker. During the Renaissance, however, the narrative sequence disappeared, leaving single paintings of the moment of shame when Adam and Eve knew they were naked. Berger makes the crucial comment that 'now their shame is not so much in relation to one another as to the spectator'. This change in viewpoint laid the basis for the tradition of the nude oil painting in which the nude female is displayed for the eyes of the viewer.

This is such a profound change that pre-Renaissance paintings look decidedly naive to the modern eye. Their symbolism, in which various colours represented various religious ideas, is lost on us. So too is much modern art which challenges the tradition of perspective and tries, against the odds, to open our eyes to other ways of perceiving the world.

But I do not want to dwell on oil painting, for although it makes the issue clear the ordinary person may not be convinced that he sees the world the same way as an oil painter does. After all, painters are supposed to be a special breed, are they not?

The world as an expression of the individual

From the Renaissance onwards people began to see the physical world around them no longer as a symbol of spiritual things (the medieval view) nor even as a purely physical agglomeration of molecules (the modern positivist view) but as *an expression of themselves*. They began to think that they could feel at home in the world only if the world reflected their personal state, their own status and achievements, their power and property, or even their transitory emotions. Chapter eight looks at the way post-Renaissance man perceives landscape in terms of ownership. This chapter looks at his perception of the world as an expression of his individual spiritual state, his character or his feelings.

Medieval people, in their more spiritual moments, considered that the world told them something about their Creator. The world was a *theophany*, the medium by which, in addition to biblical revelation, God showed himself to human beings. This view was formalized in Aquinas' 'natural theology'.

The seventeenth-century Puritan, however, began to see the environment as something which reflected his own personal state as much as the glory of the Creator. There was a tendency to see material wealth as a blessing from God, a consequence of living a moral and Christian life. This change has been classically described by the sociologist Max Weber in his *Protestant Ethic and the Spirit of Capitalism*.

A literary convention grew among Puritan writers whereby the individual's spiritual state could be expressed by describing the landscape he was travelling through. Milton, for example, in *Paradise Lost* describes the travels of the fallen angels in topographical terms:

'O'er many a dark and dreary vale

They pass'd, and many a region dolorous;
O'er many a frozen, many a fiery Alp;
Rock, caves, lakes, fens, bogs, dens and shades of death,
A universe of death.'

The whole universe is constructed by the writer in the image of the spiritual state of his characters. John Bunyan's *Pilgrim's Progress* is built entirely around this literary convention, and each road Pilgrim travels and each place he visits is explicitly symbolic of his own spiritual progress. Although the idea of pilgrimage is much older than Bunyan, definitely pre-Renaissance and pre-Reformation, Bunyan was among the first to see the landscape through which the pilgrim passed as symbolic. The medieval view, as in Chaucer's *Canterbury Tales*, sees the landscape as simply something physical to be traversed on the way to the pilgrim's goal.

With the decline of Puritanism, the tendency to see the world as a reflection of the individual's spiritual state became secularized. It became a reflection of his moral character and, later, simply his character. For example, the landscape gardeners of the eighteenth century made a conscious effort to produce a landscape that not only followed the conventions of the times but also reflected something of the ordered, rational, benevolent mind of its master. And evidently they often succeeded in this. After visiting Ralph Allen's splendid Prior Park in the early 1750s, one visitor wrote in glowing terms about his conducted tour around the grounds:

'The natural beauties of wood, water and
prospect, hill and dale, wilderness and cultivation,
make it one of the most delightful spots I ever saw
. . . I soon found those scenes animated by the
presence of the master; the tranquility and
harmony of the whole only reflecting back the
image of his own temper, and appearance of
wealth and plenty with plainness and frugality, and
yet no one envying, because all are warmed into

friendship and gratitude by the rays of his
benevolence.'

Ralph Allen was a self-made man who made his fortune by
buying up the stone quarries around Bath and selling the stone
to the speculative builders who were remaking the city. He built
his mansion on the surrounding heights looking down a V-
shaped valley into and over the city. Looking out from the
mansion, nothing is visible but the city, framed in the valley –
a landscape that embraces Allen's life and achievement. He had
translated his self into the landscape. (Looking the other way,
from the city, the mansion provided a spectacular advertisement
for his stone.)

To this day, it is assumed that a tour around a person's home
will tell the visitor much about the master or mistress of the
house; the house is taken to be a reflection of the owner. Clothes
too, are supposed not only to be functional or to reflect fashion,
but to express something about the wearer's character; likewise
handwriting. In the last decade or so, indeed, fashions in clothes
have become much more flexible, leaving much more choice to
the wearer and thus enabling greater expression of the wearer's
character. The teaching of handwriting in schools has shown a
similar lessening of the constraints of convention: no one style
is taught, and the child is allowed to develop his own style. All
this is a logical conclusion of the individualist desire to externalize his own character into physical form.

Novelists have been only too aware of this. A common way
of introducing new characters to the reader is to bring the reader
into their living room, to describe the clothes the character is
wearing, or perhaps make the first introduction through a letter
sent to some previously introduced character. To take just one
example virtually at random from the countless possibilities:
Kenneth Grahame introduces the Badger in *The Wind in the
Willows* by taking us into 'all the glow and warmth' of his
kitchen:

'The floor was well-worn red brick, and on the
wide hearth burnt a fire of logs, between two

attractive chimney-corners tucked away in the
wall, well out of any suspicion of draught. A
couple of high-backed settles, facing each other on
either side of the fire, gave further sitting
accommodations for the sociably disposed. In the
middle of the room stood a long table of plain
boards placed on trestles, with benches down each
side. At one end of it, where an arm-chair stood
pushed back, were spread the remains of the
Badger's plain but ample supper. Rows of spotless
plates winked from the shelves of the dresser at
the far end of the room, and from the rafters
overhead hung hams, bundles of dried herbs, nets
of onions, and baskets of eggs. It seemed a place
where heroes could fitly feast after victory, where
weary harvesters could line up in scores along the
table and keep their Harvest Home with mirth and
song, or where two or three friends of simple
tastes could sit about as they pleased and eat and
smoke and talk in comfort and contentment. The
ruddy brick floor smiled up at the smoky ceiling;
the oaken settles, shiny with long wear, exchanged
cheerful glances with each other; plates on the
dresser grinned at pots on the shelf, and the merry
firelight flickered and played over everything
without distinction.'

This scene of slightly austere warmth and hospitality, without
actually saying a word about Badger, clearly introduces him to
us as everyone's favourite bachelor uncle.

The introduction to Owl in *Winnie the Pooh* describes both
his home *and* his handwriting. Nor does this convention stop at
first introductions. Books such as *The Wind in the Willows* and
The House at Pooh Corner delight in describing the homes of
the various animals throughout the narrative. The fact that these
are children's books indicates that this is no esoteric convention
for readers of sophisticated adult fiction but the very language
by which we teach children to relate to their physical surround-

ings. Dickens, perhaps the most popular novelist England has produced, made his characters' houses take on the attributes of their inhabitants so that, 'each seemed perfectly suited to the other'.[3]

Not only the house but the whole landscape in which one lives can become an extension of oneself. For example, writing around 1810, the poet George Crabbe exiled his character, Peter Grimes, to a place that embodied both his objective state of rejection by the community, and his inner loneliness and desolation:

'Thus by himself compell'd to live each day,
To wait for certain hours the tide's delay;
At the same times the same dull views to see,
The bounding marsh-bank and the blighted tree;
The water only, when the tides were high,
When low, the mud half-cover'd and half-dry;
The sun-burnt tar that blisters on the planks,
And bank-side stakes in their uneven ranks.
There anchoring, Peter chose from man to hide,
There hang his head, and view the lazy tide
In its hot slimy channel slowly glide;
Where the small eels that left the deeper way
For the warm shore, within the shallows play;
Where gaping muscles, left upon the mud,
Slope their slow passage to the fallen flood;
Here dull and hopeless he'd lie down and trace
How sidelong crabs had scrawl'd their crooked race;
Or sadly listen to the tuneless cry
Of fishing gull or clanging golden-eye;
What time the sea-birds to the marsh would come,
And the loud bittern, from the bull-rush home,
Gave from the salt-ditch side the bellowing boom:
He nursed the feelings these dull scenes produce . . .'

The environment and emotions
One of the achievements of romanticism was to make the environment reflect not only the spiritual state or general character

of the perceiver but also his or her passing emotions. That something as solid as landscape should reflect something as fleeting as an individual's emotions is indeed an achievement, but the human eye is a cunning illusionist. Dorothy Wordsworth, for example, wrote in her diary on parting with her dear brother:

'The lake looked to me, I know not why, dull and
melancholy, and the weltering on the shores
seemed a heavy sound . . .'

In happier mood, a few months later while with William at the same spot:

'The lights were very grand upon the woody
Rydale hills. Those behind dark and topped with
clouds. The two lakes were divinely beautiful.
Grasmere excessively solemn and the whole lake
was calm, and dappled with soft grey ripples.'

The romantic theory of aesthetics considers that the artist interprets the landscape through his emotions, and, although it is difficult to believe that the whole long and painful process of painting a picture or composing a symphony can be sustained by the passing emotion of a moment, there is certainly plenty of evidence that romantics were considerably influenced by their feelings at the actual moment of perception. They recognized this influence, and sometimes were saddened that their melancholy perception of a scene was not how they had experienced the very same place before. Queen Victoria in her volume *More Leaves from the Journal of a Life in the Highlands* (1884), written after the death of her beloved Albert, traversed several of the mountain places that she had first explored with Albert. She describes, for example, with great precision the beauty of a late October afternoon on the moors above Balmoral. She has observed it with the accuracy of a Victorian lady of high standing who has been thoroughly trained in the observational exercise of sketching; yet her heart is not in it. It is seen as though in a dream and not real, for it does not reflect the melancholy of her inner self.

Likewise, there is a painting in the Birmingham City Gallery by Byam Shaw entitled *Boer War 1900*. A young widow in mourning stands sorrowfully in a verdant pre-Raphaelite meadow painted with all the brightness of a Constable, with the water glistening so real you can almost touch it; yet she sees nothing of this verdant beauty. Underneath the painting is a quotation from Christina Rossetti:

'Last summer green things were greener,
Brambles fewer, the blue sky bluer.'

Green things could hardly be greener than in this painting, but that is not how our heroine sees it.

In a changeable maritime climate such as Britain's, the weather is a particularly suitable candidate for the expression of emotion. For the reserved English character, the national pastime of talking about the weather provides a language in which to express one's inner moods. A sunny day enables one to say how happy one is, or to comment that one cannot share in the general rejoicing because one is a bit low. And not only do people say this, many of them actually feel this way. They feel cheated if it's a fine day and they feel low, or if it's a rainy day and they feel on top of the world. It is expected that really there ought to be some correlation between the external and the internal elements. So much so that it appears to be a statistical fact that there are more suicides in spring; it may just be tolerable to feel lousy when the weather is lousy and everyone else is complaining, but not when the weather is perking up and everyone with it, leaving behind just yourself, trapped forever in an emotional winter. Depressed people often find sunny days more difficult to manage than grey ones.

Similarly there must be no occasion worse for the young mum with the baby blues than to be out pushing her brand new chrome-plated pram, symbol of an inner joy and fulfilment which she does not feel. A more tractable part of one's immediate environment is clothes. One can swop these rather more readily than one can the weather, and so they have come to be used, and seen, not only as expressions of character but also of passing moods. Many women wear bright colours or striking patterns when they feel cheerful, or when they want to appear cheerful. Jewellery can be used similarly. One advert for diamonds says:

'These diamond stud ear-rings come with five rich
colour backings of semi-precious stone: lapiz,
black onyx, coral, malachite, and crystal. Select
the colour to match your mood and simply slide it
into position behind the diamond.'

But it is perhaps the weather that has been most used by romantic novelists to describe inner emotions. Somehow the sky, the weather and the light on the landscape have 'moods' in a way that more solid parts of the world do not. They can even express foreboding of a state that has not yet descended upon the character. Thus in *The Wind in the Willows*, Mole is stepping out in a carefree spirit to explore the wild wood, an expedition that is to prove fateful:

'It was a cold still afternoon with a hard steely sky
overhead, when he slipped out of the warm
parlour into the open air.'

Thomas Hardy is perhaps the supreme exponent of this technique.

This free literary manipulation of the elements to match our own interior state depends not only on the philosophy of individualism, but also, of course, on objective ability to control nature. So long as human society consisted of small enclaves within a hostile all-encompassing wilderness, as was the case till the middle ages in England and much later in Scotland and the United States, the elements remained something utterly intransigent, immovable except perhaps by magic. Until the idea took root that they could easily bow to human hands, it was inconceivable that they would bow to the human mind or emotions.

One still finds something of this respect for the objectivity of the elements in the Scottish writer Lewis Grassic Gibbon who described the harsh life of the tenant farmer in north-east Scotland in the first decades of this century. For his hill farmers who have only recently won some of their land from the moor, nature remains a threat that can reclaim such land only too quickly. She is a scarcely moveable force. This is a far remove from the tractable elements of Hardy's novels which reflect his characters' emotions as accurately as do Dickens' houses.

Once nature has been tamed, however, it has a distinct advantage as a vehicle for the expression of emotion. We can imagine nature to be however we desire:

'We turn towards nature. Having taken the
precaution of technologically sheltering ourselves
from most of her diseases and intemperate storms,
we embrace her as a mistress who yields to our
every fantasy because she cannot talk back, except
with the words our projections give her. In this
she is so unlike the city, so unlike politics, so
unlike people.'[4]

We can dream up whatever fantasies we like about the wilderness, because there is no one living in the wilderness who can contradict us.

In an era in which people want to project their characters and feelings onto the physical environment, interest develops not only in nature but also in the past. For the past, like nature, cannot talk back, and is therefore a subject ripe for romanticism, malleable in the image of our selves.

But some people are not content with fantasies. The architectural movement termed 'expressionism' was influential particularly in Germany in the 1920s, and may be seen elsewhere in some Rudolf Steiner communities. Its proponents believed that a building could express the mood of its builder. Thus a building like the Goetheanum is a flowing mass of curves; a smaller version of it, the Myrtle Hall near Aberdeen in Scotland, certainly has an extraordinary mood about it, and it is remarkable how its massive concrete can express an almost intangible mysticism. Concrete was the key to much expressionist architecture: it liberated the architect from the rigid form of iron that had been the basic material for the distinctly unfeeling architecture of the industrial revolution. Steiner apparently believed that you did not really need architects; anyone who had an idea could express it in a sketch which could be the basis for a building.

Clearly most buildings are not made in this expressionist fashion; similarly, not everyone feels a need for the weather to express their inner moods. The process set in train by the Renaissance has by no means reached everyone. But people do use their own homes to express individual personality in a great diversity of ways. Some of these have been suggested by the social scientists Basil Bernstein and Mary Douglas.[5] They suggest that there are two types of families, 'positional' and 'person-centered'. Positional families are those in which there is a strict hierarchy of the generations and labour is rigidly divided between the sexes. They are very structured families in which every member knows his or her place. This is reflected in the physical organization of household belongings and furnishings: everything has a place and everything is in its place. The family's strict social categories are reflected in the strictly organised physical structure of the house. A bathroom should not look like a conservatory or library any more than a husband should behave like a wife.

Person-centred families consider the individual needs of each member more important than his or her place in the family hierarchy. Members are thought of in terms of their unique personal characteristics rather than their position as father, eldest child, breadwinner or whatever. The flexibility in the way these family members relate to each other is reflected in the way they arrange their physical surroundings. The home is likely to appear much more disordered, with few clear boundaries as to what is allowed where. There may be framed prints and postcards on the bathroom wall (whereas in the positional family, the bathroom is strictly for the purpose of ablution – art appreciation is reserved for the living room). Shoes may be allowed on the kitchen table while being cleaned (whereas in the positional family, food and feet must never come into contact with the same objects). In person-centred families, the home environment tends to express the mood and character of individuals; in positional families, the environment reflects the social structure of the family.

Privacy

We all rebuild the environment around us to meet the needs of the sacred individual. Most importantly we rebuild the world to cater for our need for privacy.[6] Vast (and largely tiresome) amounts have been written about the interface between architecture, design and social psychology, most of which concentrates on issues such as crowding, privacy, territory, and personal space. The basic problem is that other people can be a pain, and architecture must somehow protect the individual from them, or at least provide places of escape.

Two features of modern houses which we take for granted, the corridor and the door, are designed precisely for this purpose.

The corridor is a relatively new innovation. The medieval peasant's house consisted of a hall with a fire in the middle; if he was a rich peasant toward the end of the period there might also have been a room upstairs. The houses of the more wealthy also consisted of a central hall, but with other rooms leading off. The very rich would have still more rooms leading off these. So in these stately homes, access to one room was through the previous one, something which any visitor to great old houses today will readily observe. A circular guided tour may take up to two hours, and not a single corridor will be traversed.

The old aristocracy did not value privacy highly. All kinds of activities could go on in the same room – sleeping, entertaining, carrying out business or politics; the king would conduct audiences from his bed. The notion of 'the private home' did not exist, for this supposes a gulf between 'society' outside one's four walls and 'private family life' which is carried on inside them. For the old-style aristocrat, society was carried on inside the great house.

It was in the sixteenth and seventeenth centuries, in the newly emerging merchant class who valued privacy much more highly, that the corridor began to emerge as a standard feature. People began to separate work from home, and one part of life from another. They lived a very ordered existence, and built their homes in such a way that each individual could carry out his allotted functions without being constantly interrupted by others passing through or engaging in incompatible activities. The corridor enabled people to move around the house without disturbing each other.

The door serves a similar function. Its purpose is not simply to keep out draughts, as is shown by the way doors are hung. Most rooms have a door near a corner, and they open toward the middle of the room, shielding the newcomer for a second from whatever the occupants of the room are doing. This provides the occupants with enough time to adjust their posture and frame of mind appropriately. It protects them from unannounced intrusions upon their privacy.

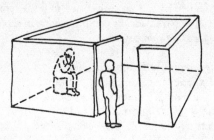

Doors and corridors not only express a culture that values privacy, but they also reinforce this value. A person growing up in a house which has doors and corridors grows to value privacy because he has never learned to do without it. For example, I grew up in a middle class home with plenty of space, one bedroom per person, a playroom and a study for homework, all of which had separate access via corridor or landing. The result is that I find it difficult to remain engrossed in what I am doing if someone else enters the room, to share a bedroom with someone, or to read a book in a room where others are doing something else. As an adult, I have therefore bought and lived in houses which have the architectural features on which I now depend. And so the chicken and egg circle of privacy and corridors proceeds around another generation. We have literally built the world in the image of the private individual.

Not everyone wants to build the world in this image, though. Open-plan living is one fashion, sponsored (I guess) by 'person-centred' families which do not want the strict division of activities implied by single-purpose rooms. And others find it difficult to build the world in the image of the private individual. They are hindered by overcrowding, neighbours, mother-in-law or the ever-instrusive telly – the whole repertoire of suburban farce. So it is that Lewis Mumford[7] complains that 'the degradation of the inner life is symbolized by the fact that the only place sacred from intrusion is the private toilet.' And affluent Americans getting tenser and tenser in their open-plan ranch-style homes may not even find that adequate: they may be attracted by the prospect of an hour ensconced in a Lilly Tank, surrounded by salt water warmed to body temperature so that no sensations whatsoever can intrude from the outside. As an ad in the *Pacific Sun* says:

'*Samadhi Isolation Tank*: Float in silence,
darkness. Experience centredness, profound
relaxation, wellbeing. Explore inner realms with
no distractions. More information and
appointments by phone. $7 per 1 hour.'

Surely here is the ultimate private environment.

Alienation from society
Privacy protects the individual from other people and even from society itself. It enables individuals to escape the seemingly all-pervading eye not only of mother-in-law, but also of arms of the state such as the taxman or the police. The way we value privacy points to an important feature of our modern belief in the individual: we do not want the individual to become totally merged into society, and we wish to distance ourselves from the

social roles by which we play our part in society. We may, like some nineteenth-century philosophers, be willing to see society as the sum total of a load of individuals, but we are not willing to see the individual as an indistinguishable component of society; that, we say, is totalitarianism or tribalism. We are prepared to define society in terms of individuals, but we resist any tendency to define individuals in terms of society. (Hence much of the antagonism to sociology and to socialism).[8]

This becomes clear perhaps if we compare our own feelings about individuality with those of traditional tribal peoples, and of pre-Reformation Europeans.

We usually talk disparagingly of ritual: 'he's merely going through a ritual', meaning we believe that his heart is not in it. There is a gulf between his outward actions, the role he is playing, and his inner self. His actions are empty conformity to what is expected of him, and do not match what he really believes. By contrast, tribal peoples seem to revel in ritual; they participate in ritual with a willingness that Westerners may enjoy as a spectacle but cannot possibly share. Such rituals are usually surprisingly flexible; there is scope for participants to vary the routine as it unfolds. The traditional and the western attitudes to ritual reveal the difference between our notions of how the self should relate to society.

In the West, the Reformation provided an important nudge toward separating the self from society and putting it on a pedestal of its own. The medieval church had advised 'good works' as the means to salvation: external actions, doing the right things, were all important. Luther and the reformers, by contrast, claimed that good works did not guarantee salvation; what mattered was the faith of the individual in his creator and redeemer. The Reformation signalled a shift away from external actions to internal faith. This created quite explosive potential for dissent between the individual and society, for the individual could be redeemed by faith in God even if his behaviour was not the kind that the authorities (religious or secular) approved of. This potential was expressed in the many religious dissenting movements of the sixteenth and seventeenth centuries. When in a later more secular age people were not so much concerned about their religious salvation, what remained was the self-authenticating individual, the person with a strong conscience, determined to stand up for his beliefs rather than submerging himself into social conformity.

Now clearly in most things people do fit in with the roles society expects of them; many people enjoy their work, they are committed mothers and fathers, they vote responsibly, and so on. But through all this 'social conformity' there runs a thread which makes each person feel that if I am to be *me*, unique me, I must somehow be more than the sum of all these parts I play. Somewhere there is a real me that is beyond, underlying, all these parts. Let us explore some of the implications this notion of 'selfhood' has for our experience of landscape.

Nostalgia for childhood

As we grow up in a complex modern society and become involved in more and more disparate activities, we all need more and more the unifying notion of a single underlying self. And as life becomes more complicated, so our memory of childhood becomes the time when life was simple and when we were 'ourselves'. So, our underlying self is revealed clearly when we recall our childhood.

Much of what has happened to me since adolescence has depended on chance meetings and choices taken: life could have turned out very differently. But my childhood, or at least what I now remember of it, is very different: it was 'given'. I present many and varied facets of myself to different audiences, but, when I think of who the *real* Julian Anthony Walter is, as like as not I am influenced by the memory of the weak, asthmatic, mathematically minded, unsporty, shy, pre-adolescent child that I was. I display few of these characteristics now, yet somehow I still think of myself as physically weak and uncoordinated, ill at ease with my peers, and good at arithmetic. This is my self-concept – wrong, but refreshingly simple.

Freud, of course, greatly encouraged us in seeing ourselves like this, persuading us that the events of early childhood determine our personalities for life. Whether or not I like my memories of childhood, they do nevertheless provide a sense of continuity to my personality which has gone through several major changes in the course of my lifetime.

Perhaps this is why we can be so nostalgic for the places where we spent our childhood, and for the sights and sounds and smells which remind us of childhood. Margaret Drabble has noted that 'most writers return again and again to childhood, seeing in a pond, a field, a tree, a church some reminder of what they once were.'[9] On the whole, places change less rapidly than people, and a return to the familiar sights of our childhood can provide concrete evidence of the reality of our childhood memories. By the same token, it can be very disconcerting to find that a place has changed out of recognition since childhood, or that the house where we grew up was demolished long ago. It is far more disconcerting than the demolition of a house in which one has lived more recently.

Smells can be particularly evocative. The smell of cigar smoke always reminds me of my father's regular Sunday evening smoke, and newly cut grass of mowing the lawn at weekends, the only time the whole family would be together. Young children smell things we adults are often oblivious to; perhaps because they are nearer the ground, perhaps because they have not come to rely on sight and sound as much as adults. Touch, taste and smell are major senses for the new-born infant. A chance encounter in later life with one of the long lost smells of childhood can bring back nostalgic memories.

The appeal of the fringes

The fact that people feel distanced from society is manifested in the attractiveness of life at the fringes – the geographical fringe (the wilderness), the historical fringe (the past), and the cultural fringe (exotic ethnic groups).

The attraction of the wilderness is not simply that it is where Nature is, but also that it is where Society is not. In the nineteenth century it was quite common for the very wealthy to build themselves tumble-down cottages to which they could retreat. Goethe described one such in the novel *Elective Affinities*, and he himself chose to live in a small and simple garden house while at the court of Weimar. Queen Victoria built a small lodge in a truly desolate location on her Balmoral estate, a lodge she visited often and spoke of with fondness.

Today, only a small minority live on the fringes, one of the more famous being Beatle Paul McCartney on his beloved Mull of Kintyre. But actually to make a living on the fringe can be a hard life. In his poem *Stone*, Alasdair Maclean wrote from his own experience of his West Highland peninsular retreat: 'God was short of earth when he made Ardnamurchan.' So, most people only *visit* rather than live on the fringes, and in so doing they make a geographical pilgrimage which reflects their social condition: normally social conformists but with a rebellious streak in them, they live their everyday suburban lives in Wembley or Westchester, or Wellington and every now and then declare their independence by breaking away to the fringes. And this is why there is a belief that in the wilderness you can find your true self, a fitting place from which the inner self can get a clear view of the society of which he is a maybe reluctant member. As one enthusiast puts it:

'It would be preferable if part of the child's
personal exploration took place in wild
countryside . . . For the wilderness is not merely
an escape from today's problems; it provides an
essential element of perspective, a time for
contemplation and self-analysis.'[10]

A place distant from society is where this inner self feels most at home. Just as the inner self (it is believed) provides a sense of perspective on the mad, hectic world, so the wilderness is believed to be the appropriate place for the contemplation and assessment of life.

Just as there is a fascination with the geographical 'out there' of the wilderness, so there is with the historical 'back there' of the past. Not that many of us would really want to live in the past – with no electricity, no efficient transport, no vote – but the semblance of the past added to the convenience of modern life is most welcome. Hence the popularity of the 'done up' olde-worlde cottage, the Georgian town house or the nineteenth-century terrace house with white iron lacework and filled with twentieth-century gadgets. In such a home, one can participate fully in modern society, while declaring symbolically that one has chosen the manners, the taste or the down-to-earthness of a previous era.

Similarly, there is a tendency to romanticize and appropriate for ourselves the culture of some minority or primitive ethnic groups. It is fashionable to have Red Indian or New Guinea carvings on the mantelpiece, a Cornish fishing net on the wall, a brass lamp from an old schooner by the front door. By injecting such objects into the home, we are declaring our independence from the mass-produced artifacts of our industrial society.[11]

Mircea Eliade has described how in religious pre-modern societies, space is divided into two:

'One of the outstanding characteristics of
traditional societies is the opposition that they
assume between their inhabited territory and the
unknown and indeterminate space that surrounds
it. The former is the world (more precisely, our
world), the cosmos; everything outside it is no
longer a cosmos but a sort of 'other world', a
foreign, chaotic space, peopled by ghosts, demons,
"foreigners".'[12]

The inhabitant of traditional societies is at home in his familiar everyday world, and terrified by the unknown. For us moderns, it sometimes seems as though the opposite is the case: we can be so disillusioned with everyday life, so alienated from it, that we imagine ourselves capable of being at home virtually anywhere else, at any historical period other than our own. We avidly read best-sellers like *The Country Diary of an Edwardian Lady*, but who would be interested in the suburban diary of a Surbiton housewife?

Virtually all societies that have ever existed have held dear their own home place and viewed foreign or unpeopled places with fear and trepidation. All, that is, apart from our own. The change was heralded by the romantic movement of the nine-teenth century, which reflected how the individual self, newly arrived on the stage of history, was alienated from society. For the first time in history, people found life in their own society not only physically hard but also morally hard. Of course, slaves, peoples occupied by invading armies and (in many societies) women have never been a part of society, but it is only recently that people who *are* full members of society have felt a distance from it, and a moral repulsion for it. Alienation from society is a typically modern phenomenon, and it has in large measure reversed our assessment of which places are 'sacred' and which 'profane'. This will be the subject of the next two chapters.

Chapter Four

SACRED AND PROFANE IN LANDSCAPE: HISTORICAL ORIGINS

'The sacred is that which the profane should not
touch, and cannot touch with impunity.'
Emile Durkheim

Gods rarely exist without demons. The religion of Nature anathematizes mankind and its ways. Individualism anathematizes
all forms of totalitarianism. The sacred implies the existence of
the profane – either that which is evil as opposed to that which
is good, or more often that which is mundane and unimportant
as opposed to that which is special. These categories of good
and bad, special and ordinary, do not exist just in the realms of
society and politics. They are manifested in the physical environment; they are given concrete form in the world around us.
They pervade the whole world, physical as well as social.

Many of the divisions into 'sacred' and 'profane' which we see
in our environment are products of the industrial revolution.
This period in history set up all kinds of dichotomies in the way
people experienced life, and these dichotomies also affected the
way they saw their physical environment.

England's eighteenth-century landowners created parklands
which divorced Nature from human civilization. But they also,
on a much bigger scale, consolidated their agricultural holdings
and improved their productivity, and this did not entail any such
divorce. The enclosing of common lands that had been going on
in England since the late Middle Ages reached its climax in the
eighteenth and early nineteenth centuries. And it was in this
period that the now typical English rural landscape of fairly

small, consolidated fields, enclosed by hedges and marked out by elms, was created. Capital was plentiful, labour was cheap, political power was monopolized by the landowning class, and change was in the air – these were the basic ingredients for the improvement of the landlord's holdings.

Early industrial undertakings fell into the same pattern as agricultural improvements. Indeed they were often not seen as being any different from these improvements. If a landowner decided to exploit the coal or iron that lay beneath his land, he was doing something no different from increasing the agricultural productivity of his land. Both the land and the minerals underneath it were resources which the landowner felt an obligation to use to the full. Many saw themselves as stewards of these resources – responsible perhaps to their heirs, perhaps to society, or perhaps to their Maker – and it was their duty to ensure that resources were not wasted.

Since industrial development was not seen as categorically different from traditional land managership, the quality of materials used and the sense of proportion and order that governed agricultural development also governed early industrial developments. An example is the architecture of the canals which were the major transportation of this period. They show a grace and elegance and fittingness to the landscape which reflect the style of their owners' Georgian homes. This is not to deny that there was ever shoddy workmanship in the building of an eighteenth-century kiln or blast furnace (the many failures of such structures indicate that there frequently was), any more than that the average labourer's cottage was a slum. But the point is that there was no gulf between standards of beauty and craftsmanship in industry and those in farming. Indeed, the workforce involved would often be interchangeable: thus a landowner might step up production from his coalmine during the winter when he could use some of his summertime agricultural labourers.

The paternalism of the early industrial entrepreneur was no different from the paternalism of the country squire. Indeed he would often be the same person, who felt he had a responsibility not only for the material resources he owned but also for his workforce. Paternalist landlords by no means totally neglected the task of building and improving the dwellings of their cottagers – with the result that the majority of the 'olde-worlde' cottages that comprise today's picture-postcard English villages date from these agricultural improvements in the eighteenth century. Industrial improvers often did likewise for their workers. The very spirit that produced the English landscape of field and village, so highly valued today for its 'pre-industrial' feel, was the same spirit that lay behind much of the early industrial 'revolution'.

This lack of dichotomy between machine and nature, industry and agriculture, may be seen in the houses not only of the workers but also of the landowners. Just as the farming landlord lived on his estate, so when he began to develop the mineral or other non-farming assets of his land there was no reason for him to move residence. A Newcomen pumping engine, or a flock of sheep grazing in newly-enclosed fields, both were fitting sights from his mansion, for both symbolized his improving condition. To use the term of the American literary historian Leo Marx, 'the machine' was quite at home in 'the garden'. So entrepreneurs stayed in close proximity to their industrial undertakings, often keeping a personal eye on, if not their day-to-day, then at least their month-by-month operation.

In their view, industry was but one more mark of the civilized mind, which could be as easily incorporated into the landscape as any other; and this confidence is reflected in early paintings of industrial works. Some artists incorporated the new works into pastoral idylls of happily-employed and contented artisans under the beneficent smile of the squire. Others, though, compared the power of forges, water-mills and steam engines to the power of nature; in the view of admirers of the sublime, both Nature and the new industry were characterized by superhuman power. An example was Burke, writing about Coalbrookdale, the cradle of the industrial revolution. In the language of Burke, 'beautiful' carries connotations of insipid and effete, while 'horrors' have a certain dramatic fascination.

'Coalbrook Dale itself is a very romantic spot, it is

a winding glen between two immense hills which
break into various forms, and all thickly covered
with wood, forming the most beautiful sheets of
hanging wood. Indeed too beautiful to be much in
unison with that variety of horrors art has spread
at the bottom: the noise of the forges, mills, and
with all their vast machinery, the flames bursting
from the furnaces with the burning of the coal and
the smoke of the lime kilns, are altogether
sublime, and would unite well with craggy and
bare rocks.'

Burke's vision of Coalbrookdale was graphically realized in several paintings, not the least being De Loutherbourg's famous *Coalbrookdale by Night* in which the almost volcanic eruption of the furnaces do indeed unite well with crags and a lone windswept tree.

The decline of paternalism

For the eighteenth-century paternalist landlord, the affairs of business and his duties as a Christian gentleman and father were one. He conducted his business as much out of a sense of duty as a desire for profit. The various aspects of his life were integrated and the landscapes he created reflected this.

But during the nineteenth century the typical entrepreneur became a man whose business operations were conducted with profit as the primary, or sole, aim. In order to provide a counterbalance to a business life dominated by economic rationality, the wife was instructed to make the home into a haven of love, dominated by all those human and Christian values absent from the market place. Thus was born the Victorian ideal of the cosy domesticity of family life.

Nor was this split between home and work confined to the families of entrepreneurs. Middle and upper class philanthropists looked with horror at the hundreds of thousands of women factory workers and their children who were doing in the factories what they had done for generations previously at home: combining work with motherhood, labour with play. Philanthropists considered that the proper place for all women to be was at home looking after their children. So the reformers initiated moves to get first the children of the poor and then their mothers out of the factories and into the home where they belonged. They attempted to make the proletarian family an image of their own bourgeois families, with the man at work supporting his wife and children at home.

So were introduced the present-day dichotomies between the world of men and the world of women, and between the world of adults and the world of children. And these dichotomies became reality partly through being embodied in the physical environment. The factory owners moved as far away as possible, upwind, from their factories. For those who could afford it, home and work were separated physically as well as socially, and the world of women and the world of men were physically separated too.

This may be one origin of the fact, consistently revealed by researchers, that boys and girls are expected to relate to their environment differently. Boys are allowed to play further from home than girls. They are expected to explore and conquer the world, and even to break the distance rules set for them by their parents ('boys will be boys'), whereas little girls are expected to stay at home and be domestic. Girls play with stable, ordered, *interior* scenes (dressing up dolls, and so on), while boys play with *exterior* scenes (toy cars, trainsets, and so on) and have a particular concern with collapse and downfall: ruins are exclusively boys' constructions.

The psychoanalyst Erik Erikson sees these differences as a reflection of boys' and girls' anatomies; the womb for girls and the penis for boys shape their experience not only of their own bodies but of all space. An alternative explanation seems more plausible to me in the light of modern research. Children are encouraged in such different patterns by adults as a differential preparation for the outside work role (male) and the home-based domestic role (female) which they will be expected to play as adults. If this is so, then it would seem that the *social* division between home and work that became the norm as a result of the industrial revolution has had a profound effect on how boys and girls, men and women, experience space.

Described thus far, men and women have different, but equally moral and valuable, parts to play. But there is an important dichotomy not only in the roles that men and women play but also in the evaluation of these roles. The role of the male breadwinner came to be seen as the more practical in that without bread the household starved; and in this stark economic accounting the value of the woman's work in the home was curiously discounted. Further, because politics was part of the public world, while women held sway over the private world, women were excluded from politics even as the franchise was being extended to more and more men. Thus arose the belief that men were needed to run the country, while women were not competent for the affairs of state.

But, while the *practical* indispensability of men was accepted, the wife and mother was being put on a pedestal of a moral and aesthetic, rather than a practical, kind. Women, it was imagined, had the saintly power of delivering their menfolk from the corruption of public life and from the degradation of factory work. A vase of flowers at home made up for the brutality of the factory, and reminded the man that there was more to life than the wage packet; or at least that was the theory of the Victorian bourgeois family. Crucially, this ideology justified a division in the understanding of *beauty*: it was justifiable for factories to be ugly, noisy and dangerous because they were dominated, and should be dominated, by the rule of money. Love, joy and beauty were the guiding motifs in the feminine world of the home, and it was here that one expected to find the vase of flowers, the little bit of love and the little bit of beauty provided without any eye for the economic return. So, whereas the architecture of eighteenth-century canals, factories and country homes were all of a piece, there emerged a dramatic aesthetic gulf between the factories and the homes of the factory owners in the mid-nineteenth century. A divorce had been set up between beauty and money, between aesthetics and economics, between consumption and production, between the world of women and that of men. This divorce lies at the heart of the blight on our landscape which many deem to be the legacy of the industrial revolution. Entrepreneurs were ceasing to love the workplaces and the workscapes they were responsible for building, retreating for nourishment of their aesthetic sensibilities to havens of beauty called 'home'. They were destroying a landscape which had been all of a piece, and were consciously and systematically building a landscape which was basically profane but interspersed by sacred pockets of rest and beauty. This is still the basis of our thinking about landscape.

These pockets of sylvan beauty were largely created in the newly emerging suburbs of the middle classes who were more than glad to remove themselves as far as possible from the slums of the workers. The social, political and economic gaps which separated the newly emergent classes of bourgeoisie and proletariat were made manifest in an all-too obvious geographical gap between the suburbs and the slums. The aspiring middle classes wanted to get away from the *dirt* – moral as well as physical – of the labouring poor, which is why for the bourgeoisie 'cleanliness was next to godliness'. The preoccupation with dirt and its elimination at this time *preceded* any knowledge about germs. Cleanliness was a way in which the new middle class family, with no inherited wealth or status of its own, could distinguish itself from the lower orders. Middle class housewives instructed their maids to keep scrubbing the floor, to create an ordered, clean environment in the home which clearly marked it off from the profane world outside.

Social class and the environment

Medieval society had been composed of very clearly defined social groups or 'estates'. Social distinctions were so strict that it was virtually impossible to move from one estate to another: once a priest, always a priest; once a baron, always a baron; once a serf, always a serf. Everyone knew these distinctions so well that it did not matter that *physically* people were all jumbled up together. The knight on his horse and the beggar jostled for space in the same crowded street, for there were no pavements; master craftsman and apprentice slept in the same room, perhaps even in the same bed. People's notion of their station in life was so fixed that the social order easily survived the physical proximity of social unequals. One found the same sort of physical proximity up till 1865 in the southern USA, where the black slave might dress and undress the master or mistress.

The industrial revolution finally marked the change from a society composed of static estates to a (theoretically) fluid, competitive society made up of social classes in which the aim was to move up from one class to the next. This blurred the social divisions between people, a process which has accelerated in the twentieth century. Universal education and the vote for everyone mean that it can be hard to ascertain someone's social position, especially if a wide range of social classes shop at the same superstores.

The decline of strict social divisions in society has led to increasing reliance on *physical* divisions as markers. In the nineteenth century, those who could afford it appropriated private space for themselves in the suburbs to demarcate themselves from the labouring classes. The nouveaux riches were, and still are, particularly anxious to announce their new station in life through visible display: a better house, a bigger garden, in a better area. The oft-noted vulgarity of the taste of the nouveau riche derives from just this need to exaggerate his appearance of wealth, to hit others in the eye with it and make sure they do not forget. The long established titled man, by contrast, can be subtle and refined in his taste: everyone *knows* his position in life, and he does not have to prove it to anyone.

Those who did not have the resources to appropriate a mansion in the country or a house in the suburbs still faced the problem of how to distinguish themselves physically from others. After houses, clothes and hairstyle were the next best means of expressing social position. They have been particularly important at certain times for the self image of largely property-less groups such as the lower class, blacks and teenagers. Think of the British working class family who take great pride in their 'Sunday best', the dandily dressed American black, the range of youth subcultures in Britain from the teddy boys of the 1950s to the punks of the 1980s. You would not find any of these going about in a sloppy old sweater like the aristocrat or the well-born hippy.

For those with nothing to their name, the care of the body is always a final means of distinguishing oneself from social inferiors. This raises the interesting question of why Americans, the most affluent of people, should be so pre-occupied with the care of their bodies. While it clearly has a lot to do with their infatuation with health and youth, there may also be a less discussed reason. Americans do not believe social class exists; they believe all people to be born equal and of equal worth. Yet at the same time they live in a competitive society in which one has to prove one's worth. Since not everyone can own a Cadillac or a tasteful residence, most Americans are in need of more available means for keeping up appearances. Though cosmetics and yoga are not exactly free, they are within the financial reach of the vast majority. Keeping the body beautiful is one way an American retains respect in his or her own and others' eyes. In a society where social divisions are believed to be minimal, physical separateness becomes ever more important. Ultimately, the final way to protect one's identity from 200 million other equals is to retreat to the wilderness, away from them all. Inhabitants of nations with a more fixed social order do not have such identity problems.

A curious thing has happened. People have moved away from the land in their millions in the last two centuries, and one would have expected people therefore to be less attached to *place*. No longer are we involved with the soil, with a particular patch of this earth. Yet at precisely the same time, it has become more and more important to display ourselves and our station in life through material goods and through that part of our environment – however small – which is under our control, whether it be suburban garden, motor car, or dress and body care. Control over our physical environment has become crucial in the fight against descent into the profane world of our social inferiors.

The discovery of the countryside

The industrial revolution did something to tools. Simple tools do not cut the operator off from the materials he is operating on: the gardener with his spade feels as much in contact with the soil as the child scrabbling in it with his hands. The spade mediates between him and the soil, it does not cut him off from the soil. It is the means by which he feels in his aching back the difference between wet clay and dry loam. But once power tools became available – power based not on the eccentricities of wind, water or animals – the tool became the machine, and it cut the operator off from his materials. *He* operates the machine, and *the machine* operates on the materials. In some industries such as coalmining this change has come about only relatively recently, and in a few, notably the building of single houses by small building firms, hardly at all.

So a separation grew between workers and natural materials. To this may be added the division of labour; the worker does not experience his labour as residing within the final product, and the consumer never meets the person who originally handled the raw materials. Today we are surrounded by a world of artefacts whose material origins we have little idea of. This has greatly accentuated the distinction between Man and Nature which goes back as far as the late middle ages.

This was most clearly manifest in the newly emergent distinction between the city and the country. Until the nineteenth century, all towns had been small enough not to lose visual contact with the countryside. As commercial centres (Norwich, Bristol, London, New York, Boston) or market towns they were thoroughly integrated into a basically rural economy, an integration nostalgically portrayed in Hardy's *The Mayor of Casterbridge*. This location of the city as an element within a basically rural landscape is illustrated by that genre of painting which viewed a city from the rising ground of the neighbouring countryside; the city appears as completely surrounded by countryside. This style went out of fashion sometime in the mid-nineteenth century, not because such views were no longer obtainable (even today you can see right across Glasgow, Bristol and Edinburgh) but because they were no longer believable.

In the nineteenth century the town replaced the village as the place of residence of the vast majority of the population. For the first time since ancient Rome, there were cities with populations of over a million, and the typical citizen lived in a world composed of streets and bricks and mortar, with 'the countryside' being something alien out there. The town has continued to be painted, but not from without, as in the broad vista, but from within as in the paintings of Lowry. The countryside has continued to be painted, but as a pretty object out there, categorically different from the city. No major artist today, in Britain or America, attempts to show any kind of balance between the two.

The countryside has become something to be visited. At the very time that technology cut people off from the countryside, technology also came up with a revolutionary mode of transport – the railway (and later the automobile) – which enabled the urban masses to rediscover the countryside in a new mode, the mode of leisure. From the Victorian factory worker's hard-earned day-trip to the seaside to today's flood of automobiles to the nearest national park each public holiday, the trip to the country has become an enduring part of modern culture. The countryside has become something essentially different, not operating – the towny supposes – according to the ordinary laws of capitalism, industry and economics, but according to the norms of nature, of a past age, of aesthetics. It has become an anomalous and curious art object to be visited and enjoyed during those anomalous periods of time called leisure.

This compartmentalizing of space is matched by the urban dweller's compartmentalizing of *time*. Time is composed of the working week plus a few residual pockets called 'leisure time'.[1] What more appropriate time, then, to visit the countryside than leisure time, for both are 'left over' from the real business of life in a modern industrial society.

From work ethic to leisure ethic
Industrial society holds work in high esteem and uses it as an important way of sustaining the individual's sense of identity. Yet the notion is gaining more and more ground[2] that leisure is

when real life is to be lived. This notion sums up several of the trends discussed so far in this and the previous chapter. Leisure is enjoyed typically within the private circle of the family and is regarded as the area where one's real self can express itself. It is welcomed as a respite from the world of work in which one pays one's debt to society. It is the time when I can be the real me, rather than the alienated me that I am all too often in my role as factory worker, office worker or housewife. Leisure time takes on a sacred aspect, in contrast to the profane mundane time in which obligations to society, and possibly to family, are fulfilled.

Since this real self is believed to be found particularly in leisure *time*, leisure *places* are more likely to be sacred than work places. There can be magic in places visited in leisure time, but rarely is there any magic in the place of work. The other day, during the course of my part-time work as a builder's labourer, I was working on an olde-worlde cottage in a charming setting in the heart of the Cotswold hills, and was enjoying my tea break in the high summer sun. It was pleasant, but not magical. Also enjoying the sun was a friend of the owner on a few day's break from her dismal basement flat and hectic job in the neighbouring conurbation. For her these precious moments were transparently magical. The place was sacred for her because her treasured leisure was sacred; it was pleasant enough for me as a place to work, but hardly magical. If I think of the few places on earth which have embodied for me my image of paradise, they are all places I have visited in the course not of my work but of my leisure – even though I have worked in places others might deem of equal beauty.

Part of the reason for this is that since the eighteenth century we have come to believe that one cannot admire the beauty of something while one is involved in practical activity. If there is a fine sunset, you have to stop work if you are to enjoy it. The useful cannot be beautiful; mammon and beauty cannot go together. I have already mentioned that this notion was initiated in landscape terms by the landscape gardeners of the eighteenth century who found their unproductive landscaped parklands and their picturesque grottoes and waterfalls far more beautiful than their productive farmlands. The idea was carried into every middle class Victorian home via the notion that home and garden, the economically useless sphere of consumption, were to be lovingly made beautiful to compensate for the ugliness of the factory, the economically useful sphere of production. This view of aesthetics, together with its eighteenth-century origins, has been described as follows:

'It has become a commonplace of aesthetics today
that appreciation of beauty requires a
'disinterested' attitude of attention, a state of mind
in which we are absorbed in the object presented,
in becoming fully and completely aware of the
object itself without being deflected by concern for
its practical and utilitarian implications. But in the
eighteenth century the idea was a new one. The
word 'disinterested' did not, of course, imply lack
of interest in the object of attention but the
absence of any 'self-interest', any considerations of
advantage or utility, and indeed any interest at all
other than the direct contemplation of the object
and satisfaction achieved from our awareness of
it.'[3]

Leisure, then, is required for the admiration of beauty, not least of beautiful places.

This philosophy is so completely accepted[4] that virtually all modern nations have considered that each individual finding his own 'magic' place is not enough. They have designated certain places as especially beautiful and to be dedicated to the so-called leisure needs of the whole population. All modern nations have set aside national parks, areas of outstanding natural beauty, national forests, wilderness areas, conservation areas, historic sites and heritage sites (only the names vary from country to country). These special places tend to be economically useless. National parks are almost invariably in the wildest, agriculturally least productive landscapes that a nation possesses. Historic buildings, in their preserved state, are typically inappropriate for modern uses. When such places *do* have practical uses, bitter conflict typically ensues, their utilitarian role and their role as sacred shrine being deemed incompatible. The current debate about flooding the Franklin River in south-west Tasmania, one of the few remaining 'wild' rivers in the world, for a proposed extension to the State's hydro-electric scheme is a case in point.

The planning legislation governing these places is special: strict aesthetic standards are applied to them, while in more mundane places planners are generally required to be concerned not with aesthetics but with the technical criteria of safety, housing density, traffic flow, and so on.

The land has become degraded aesthetically, mundane and profane, but dotted with sacred islands of beauty and meaning. This landscape reflects a society in which everyday life tends to be meaningless, but from which one regularly escapes in order to be oneself. The modern self, its individuality and authenticity, is held in such historically unprecedented esteem that I term it sacred; and so the places to which the individual goes in order to be him or herself in turn become sacred and in need of state protection. Only thus can one comprehend why the USA, that most ardent opponent of socialism, should also be the most ardent exponent of the national park, which involves the nationalizing of land on a massive scale. For it is in the States that the individual is most nearly sacred, and so it becomes crucially important to safeguard these shrines for the leisurely re-creation of the human self, battered by a tense and competitive society.

In the next chapter I propose to look in a little more detail at some features of sacred places and profane places, but first it is perhaps worth summarizing what I have described so far. The dichotomies which arose from the industrial revolution have been objectified in the landscape, translated from social concepts to embodiments in the physical environment.

SACRED		PROFANE	
social concept	environmental embodiment	social concept	environmental embodiment
private home woman consumption	the house	public business man production	the factory
bourgeoisie	suburb (clean)	proletariat	slum (dirty)
nature	countryside	machine	city
leisure real me	national parks	work alienated me	everyday environment

Chapter Five

SACRED AND PROFANE IN LANDSCAPE: CONTEMPORARY PROBLEMS

The modern view of aesthetics is that disinterestedness is a prerequisite for the appreciation of beauty. This *can* be taken to mean that *any* object can be appreciated aesthetically, once we have detached ourselves from wordly concerns and viewed the object 'in the aesthetic mode'. Black and white photography has done us a great service here: by abstracting the elements of texture, light and form from objects, views and places which in our everyday experience are mundane if not ugly, photography has enabled us to view the most mundane of places in an aesthetic light.

But this is not how beauty is normally conceived today. Rather we have decided that beauty resides not in a particular way of seeing, but in a particular class of objects: objects that have no use value and that have been deemed by 'experts' to be 'works of art'. As Harold Osborne puts it 'The concept of the "fine arts" was based on the idea of a class of artefacts constructed solely or primarily for the purpose of being contemplated aesthetically.'[1] A very few artefacts are considered works of art, set like pearls in the mere ordinary stuff of life. In our culture, works of art possess something of the sacred; they are wholly other from ordinary artefacts, and are produced by an extraordinary breed of human beings called artists. 'Geniuses' produce 'masterpieces' of a totally different order from the paintings of amateur dabblers – a different order reflected in the prices the two kinds of paintings fetch. These assumptions have been challenged by people like Andy Warhol and the punks, but so far they do not seem to have been particularly successful in persuading people of their view that art should be both for and by everyman.

The dominant notion of the special art object has now been extended from specially-produced single objects to entire landscapes, as Margaret Drabble suggests in her phrase 'landscape as art'. There are two prime candidates for this appellation: historic places and rural places. History and rurality are the twin genii of landscape art, producing landscapes that our modern urban culture cannot hope to aspire to, and that therefore must be preserved. If it were possible, doubtless the guardians of the 'national heritage' would encase them in glass to make sure everyone appreciated them as art.

This creates problems for those who happen to live in places that are designated primarily 'for aesthetic contemplation'. You can't spend your whole life aesthetically contemplating the place where you live, unless perhaps like Wordsworth you happen to make a living out of poetry. This means that in his everyday business the resident is out of tune with the place. For example, I live in the city of Bath, built with great architectural panache for leisured and wealthy visitors of the eighteenth century. Bath is perhaps as near as you can get to a complete town built as a work of art. Designed to be aesthetically contemplated in the course of leisurely strolls, it is very difficult to appreciate while hurrying to get the shopping done; but I certainly can and do enjoy it when I'm off duty and can stroll around, perhaps in the company of some visiting friends, at my leisure. I know I am not alone in this 'double vision', and doubtless those who have to make a living in national parks like the Lake District find much the same. By contrast in Aberdeen, North Sea oil boom town of the 1970s where I lived before, I most definitely could and did appreciate the townscape and the architecture as I dashed to do the shopping. The profane nature of my travels within the city as a resident was in tune with the profane business and busy-ness of the city, and my senses consequently felt at home there and open to beauty where it was to be found. (This may be why those who retire to their beloved shangri-las of former holidays are often sadly disappointed with them as permanent homes.)

But Bath is an exception. The vast bulk of the English countryside and historic places like olde-worlde villages, thatched cottages and the Tower of London were not built as works of art. They were constructed for much more practical purposes, so how can they now be dubbed works of art? This problem lies right at the heart of the concept of a work of art as something 'constructed solely or primarily for the purpose of being contemplated aesthetically'. Prior to the eighteenth century when this concept was invented, few if any objects were constructed primarily for aesthetic contemplation. The medieval icon was to aid spiritual devotion, the oil portrait of the Umpteenth Earl of Puddlingham was intended to hang in the ancestral home to make manifest the ancestral line, and so forth. But this does not prevent us now dubbing them 'works of art'. The trick is to abstract them from the utilitarian, political or religious context in which they were produced. This can be done either by literally transporting them from the cathedral or ancestral hall to the art gallery (or even more dramatically by carting the stones of ancient Greek temples and statues to the British Museum) or by letting the passage of time lull us into ignorance of their original purpose, so that even though they still be viewed in situ we see them solely in aesthetic terms.

Exactly the same trick of decontextualization enables the complex reality of the countryside and of historic buildings to be reduced to objects of art. The trick is to abstract from their complexly intertwined utilitarian, political and religious reality one particular aspect – the visual – and to make that represent the true reality of these places. The village and the castle become things to be *looked at*, visually beautiful objects that simply exist. They are by no means to be represented as *products*, products of human labour, of political intrigue or of religious devotion, for this would detract from their status as works of art.

The past and the countryside, specially marked out for enjoyment, do not even function as museums, for museums should inform and educate. And this is the one thing the worshipped past countryside cannot do, for by being represented purely visually, they are fundamentally falsified. To inform the visitor that these places are the product of ordinary human beings acting out of very ordinary motives would be to destroy their character as sacred and as works of art. A veneer of supposed information may be supplied, as in the increasingly common visitor centres and guide books, but the very existence of a visitor centre implies that a place is special, perhaps even sacred. Factual information is overwhelmed by glossy colour photographs. Even in visitor centres where the actual view may be seen out of the window there is a predominance of colour photographs; these function to tell the visitor that primarily he should prepare himself for a *visual* experience.

Representing the visual as the essence of such locations causes further problems for those who have the misfortune to live in them. If you are to live in a place, it must serve all your daily needs: for work, for domestic convenience, for socializing, for mobility, and so forth. But in our culture art objects are not supposed to have anything to do with such utilitarian needs. Bath, for example, internationally known as a beautiful city and famed for its Georgian architecture, yearly attracts hundreds of thousands of visitors who come to see a pretty place. The city council's consequent expenditure on flowers and other means of prettifying the streets, in preference to providing housing for the local population or improving the amenities of the lesser-known neighbouring industrial communities that have not been dubbed 'pretty', do not endear the council to many of Bath's citizens who have to live in the place. Even closer to home, I live in a very ordinary Georgian terraced building which, like virtually all others in the city, is under a preservation order because of its architectural and historic importance. I have therefore been denied permission to add a window to the facade to light a bedroom that has never had (by today's standards) proper illumination. My house has been declared a work of art, and my sin is wanting to see it as a home fit for living in. Actually, I also enjoy living in a Georgian dwelling; but when it comes to the crunch, the law says that the definition of the house as an art object preserved for the nation takes precedence over its definition as a dwelling for the individual resident.

Examples can be cited by the hundred. Residents of English and Welsh national parks who simply want to make a decent living, continually find themselves thwarted, even though it was their ancestors doing just this that created the landscape now deemed a work of art. Let me cite just one more example with which I am personally acquainted. In a Gloucestershire village that has been designated a conservation area and that is also within a much larger 'Area of Outstanding Natural Beauty' (a kind of grade II national park), a local man applied for permission to convert a shed into a jewellery workshop in which he and three apprentices would work. Given the rapid conversion of such villages to dormitories for nearby towns and given the lack of employment opportunities for local young people who are thereby forced to leave the village, one would think this application would be welcomed by the authorities. Not so. Application refused: 'area not scheduled for industrial development'. Enter once again the deep-rooted legacy of the industrial revolution, namely that industry is by definition ugly and can pose nothing but a threat to art objects such as a pretty village.

Anxiety over profanation
This brings us to an important feature of sacred places: they are invariably surrounded by fears that they will be profaned. There is always the danger that the profane will touch the sacred and defile it.

To prevent the profane city engulfing the sacred countryside, 'green belt' policies have been widely adopted in Britain since the 1940s, ringing cities with bands of countryside which cannot be built on. The thinking behind green belt policies has nowhere been better described than by Emile Durkheim, who was at the time actually describing the religion of Australian Aborigines:

'The sacred thing is par excellence that which the profane should not touch, and cannot touch with impunity . . . Sacred things are those which the interdictions protect and isolate; profane things,

those to which these interdictions are applied and
which must remain at a distance from the first.'[2]

The sacred is the source of power, but it is also inherently
vulnerable to contact with the profane.

This helps account, I think, for another phenomenon. The
presence of large trucks thundering through olde worlde towns
and villages has become a highly emotive issue in Britain in
recent years. These juggernauts are symbols of the profane
industrial world which policies such as the green belt should
have kept in its place, firmly separated from the sacred olde
worlde villages. While heavy goods were transported by rail,
there *was* this separation, for the railways largely bypassed old
residential areas. But the arrival of the juggernaut suddenly
brought the industrial revolution literally to the front door of
everyman. Here it was on the very threshold of the private home
which since Victorian times had been eulogized as a haven of
rest from the industrial world. And worse still, some of these
homes were among the prettiest in all Britain, so residents and
national preservation organizations joined hands to resist the
juggernaut.

Pollution is not ultimately to do with physical intrusions such
as fumes and noise and eyesores, but with the crossing of proper
boundaries. Pollution is identified not when decibels and smells
reach unacceptable levels, but when something is identified as
having exceeded its bounds and being in the wrong place. A
juggernaut pulling out of the factory gate is not deemed pollut-
ing, but the same vehicle roaring past the half-timbered, ivy-
covered Tudor inn overlooking the village green is.

Or to give another example. The modern dairy farm has as
much impact on the immediate environment as the typical factory, if not more. It affects virtually all the senses: the sight of
the modern concrete and corrugated-iron milking parlour resem-
bles a factory building, the noise of the milking machine starts
at 5 a.m., the smell is distinct, and the excreta of the cows litter
the lane along which neighbouring residents have to walk in
order to get home. In addition, tankers too big for British
country lanes come daily to collect the milk, the delays to traffic

caused by the herd can be considerable, and cows wander onto unprotected front gardens. Such incursions on the environment would be deemed intolerable pollutions by neighbours of most factories, yet I have never heard villagers or planners define these aspects of the dairy farm as pollution. The reason is that dairy farms are deemed appropriate to the countryside, even to the heart of villages, while factories with considerably less environmental impact are not. At root, the offence of the proposed factory in an English village is not that it is noisy, ugly, or smelly, but that it is out of place. Pollution is essentially profanation: the bringing of the profane into contact with the sacred.

The national park may be understood as America's dramatic solution to the problem of profanation. Unlike the frail strip of green belt, the national park is protected by its immensity and its distance from the industrial world. It is a protection of the sacred by sheer distance. And in the still more protected 'wilderness areas' the defence is made even more sure by the banning of the road, that major route by which the profane industrial world penetrates other sacred places.

But even national parks are not free of what the political scientist Lincoln Allison[3] has called 'environmental neurosis', the fear of profanation. For the discovery of important mineral deposits within such a park is bound to lead to pressure for their exploitation. In Australia, multinational companies have even lobbied State and Federal government for mining rights to the Great Barrier Reef, an offshore national 'park', and for the sand mining of Fraser Island, an ecologically fragile environment to its south. Allison's complaint is that environmental neurosis, the fear that nothing is sacred, leads to every proposed development in any setting, special or not, being opposed by preservationists. Allison's proposal is to designate certain places as truly sacred; they would not be touched under *any* circumstances. But it seems to me that this is exactly what we have been trying to do for 150 years, and is the cause rather than the solution of the problem. Not only does this approach tend to make life intolerable for those few who have to live in the sacred shrines, but it also tends to release the rest of the land into the clutches of profanity.

Profane places

As rural villages and historic towns become prettier and prettier, more and more like (rather uninformative) museums, and as higher and higher aesthetic standards are demanded of them, so the contrast between these sacred places and the profane environment in which most of us have to live gets wider. Not that ordinary towns and suburbs are necessarily getting uglier – probably the reverse – but the gap between them and special places is widening. While aesthetic criteria increasingly govern planning decisions in national parks and conservation areas, no such scrutiny applies to developments in ordinary places.

Thus the *belief* that beauty should reside pre-eminently only in certain selected places is becoming *reality*, which in turn is generating the desire for such places. This is an important point, and provides a suitable occasion to emphasize a major theme in this book. By describing our dealings with the environment as 'religious', I am not referring to a set of *attitudes* which we as individuals are free to accept or reject. The essentially religious meanings we give to places have become part of the actual physical environment in which we have to live; subjective belief has become objective reality, and therefore demands a response. This religious dimension will not go away simply by our ignoring it. The meaning given to a place by people becomes part of the place.

This oversimplifies the case however, for there are beliefs which have not become embedded in the actual physical environment, and some of these still manage to affect our experience of the environment profoundly. For example, the belief that English country villages should be beautiful has not yet entirely come about; one consequence of the banning of even small industries from such villages is that they have become less and less like villages and more and more like dormitory suburbs. A row of half-timbered cottages knocked into one, with a couple of expensive cars parked outside does not fool anyone, and hardly represents the close-to-nature rural paradise that people seek.

The myth of the ugly town

The corollary of the belief that beauty exists only in special places is the myth that beauty cannot exist in the ordinary places in which most people live. This is tragic, for it blinds people to the very real beauty that exists in even the most mundane of places, and it dulls their vision of what the city could be like. The problem is that our standards for beauty are derived from the 'sacred' places. These standards are passed on to the lay person in three particular ways, by photography, by the tourist trade and by transport.

Although, as I have already said, sophisticated black-and-white photography has done a great service in revealing the beauty in the cooling tower, the puddle of water on the bomb-site, or the pylons on the horizon, these are not the sort of photographs which chiefly surround us. Rather we are inundated with the glossy brochure, the countryfied television advert for wholemeal bread, the full-colour calendar pictures of English villages, natural wonders of the world, tranquil forests and streams, and so on. These are not imaginative revelations of beauty in the mundane; rather they are stereotyped visions of what special places ought to be like. Now even in the days of oil paintings, artists falsified the landscapes they painted; they painted in a given style, perhaps making an English field look as though it were a classical Italian landscape. However, people knew that real English fields did not look like that. But the camera, we moderns believe, cannot lie. So when we see a calendar photograph or picture postcard of an English village with not a telegraph pole or motor car in sight, we believe it. The photograph is as contrived as the oil painting, but it hides the contrivance and is thus doubly false. It is dishonest about its dishonesty.

This covert idealizing of sacred landscapes has at least two consequences for how we perceive the environment. Firstly, when we visit such places we are disappointed. This is not because the place is not like it was thirty years ago, because generally we do not know what it was like thirty years ago. Rather it is because it is not like it was in the picture. The picture did not show other tourists, it did not show litter and ice cream vans, it did not show motor cars. This is perhaps why tourists are preoccupied with taking a picture themselves from the one angle that omits these undesirable features, for then in their memory the place will look like their pre-formed image of it. The aim is to make the place look like the photograph.

Secondly, through this process of looking at and taking colour photographs, people come to take into themselves the stereotyped images of what is beautiful. This then forms the (totally inappropriate) standard by which they judge their own environment when they go home. And if you want proof, just wander around an English suburban street and look at how people try to remake their homes in these stereotyped images: half-timbered gables, neo-Georgian doors, glazing bars and chunky glass in bow windows. Or look inside their homes, and compare the number of idealized prints and photographs of sacred places with the number of genuinely artistic photographs revealing beauty in their own street.

The tourist industry provides explicit signposting as to what is worth looking at and what isn't, what is beautiful and what isn't. When I visited Birmingham recently I went to the city information bureau to see if they had anything on Birmingham. I could not find a single brochure among the dozens on the shelves, though I could take my pick of any number of exotic islands in the Caribbean or stately homes in the nearby countryside. Clearly the office was there to entice Brummies out of Birmingham, not to show visitors, let alone Brummies, what treasures there were in England's second city. So, meekly, I enquired at the counter, saying I was interested in the Victorian city-centre buildings which were built when Birmingham was the workshop of the world. The girl seemed optimistic that she could help and, after a minute or so burrowing behind the counter, handed me just what I wanted – a quite superb leaflet guiding me round the buildings of architectural and historic importance in central Birmingham; and a fascinating tour it turned out to be. So somebody in the Birmingham City Council had some imagination, but bless their hearts they were not exactly going out of their way to tell people about Birmingham in the way that they told people about Paris, Glencoe and the Grand Canyon. Who but a slightly odd author like me would want to explore a profane place like Birmingham?

The progress of this myth, which says that the further you go from home the more likely you are to find beauty, is made much easier by mass transport. Without the railway and aeroplane, and most certainly without the motor car, people who want to get out of the house would have to explore their immediate neighbourhood on foot, which indeed is what the Victorian family did on its Sunday afternoon outings. But with the aid of the motor car, the modern family rushes oblivious past unknown treasures near to home on its headlong way to some well advertized regional or national shrine.

It is instructive to compare my appreciation and knowledge of my local environment with my two nearest neighbours. One has a car and frequently reports to me enthusiastically about the super old mill or village or inn which they have just discovered only half an hour's drive away. I, without a car, nod sagely, knowing equally pretty places a mere half hour's walk away. But my other neighbour had the last laugh; over sixty and with a very short-legged dog, she discovered a few yards from the house things and people which I stride past as boldly as my other neighbours drive past.

But, you may say, living in Bath means it's all very well to talk about beauty a few minutes' walk from my doorstep; most Britons do not live in such aesthetically privileged places but in vast soulless conurbations. Of course, there are a few places where local beauty is precious hard to find. But most towns and cities contain humanly made beauty which is all too often overlooked in the rush to the countryside. In addition, I have been surprised at how easily the beauty of nature can be found in most of Britain's biggest cities. The city need not cut us off from nature, as the myth would have it, and there are several geographical reasons for this:

The sea. Perhaps half of Britain's large towns are seaports. A walk along the seafront on a stormy February night is as close as most people would ever want to get to nature in the raw.

Rivers. Most towns are built on rivers; these often provide veins of countryside entering the city, or arteries by which the town dweller may escape to the country. Oxford (population 100,000) is a classic example.

Steep valleys. Several of the industrial towns of Lancashire and Yorkshire lie in valleys. These often have wooded side valleys, too steep to build on, which are usually sheltered from the noise of the city and provide the welcome sound of falling water. In Sheffield (population 700,000) you can walk from within a mile of the city centre right out onto the moors along a secluded glen of this kind.

Surrounding hills, like the sea, provide a clear boundary to the city and remind the city dweller that freedom and wildness are close to hand. The classic examples in Britain are Glasgow (population 1 million), and Edinburgh (population 500,000).

Canals share with secluded glens the advantage of insulation from the noise of the city. Often sited below the general ground level of the city, they provide peace and quiet and wildlife in the very heart of the city:

'I remembered how on an April evening Fred had rowed us dreamily along part of the Regent's Canal. Overhead the buds were breaking on the elms, the rooks were cheerfully sorting themselves into pairs. My wife and I sat in the stern of the dinghy, she trailing her fingers in the water and I myself looking up dreamily at the silhouette of the trees against the evening sky, amazed that such peace and beauty could exist right there in London. Only thirty feet above us the traffic was jammed motionless on Blow-up Bridge, but it seemed to belong to another world, incredibly remote. And so it did.'[4]

Occasionally a village remains intact within the city boundary.

Aberdeen (population 200,000) for example, contains two: the fishing village of Footdee and the ancient hamlet of Balgownie.

The British city most lacking in such features is London, though it does contain a river and some canals. This happens also to be the city where most of the opinion-formers live: politicians, civil servants, media people, advertisers, and so forth. *Their* experience of the urban environment is that it consists of unrelieved bricks and mortar, with the countryside a rare and precious anomaly; these are the people who think up ideas such as national parks, who locate sacred nature as far away from the city as possible. It is easy for the Londoner to think that all cities are like London, only smaller. (I think I have a right to say this since I am myself a Londoner born and bred, and used to think this way.)

Whether American cities also possess these natural features in such profusion is debatable. Certainly some do. Chicago (population 7 million), with America's best skyscrapers, dramatically fronts onto Lake Michigan, creating one of the finest juxtapositions of raw nature with urban landscape to be found anywhere in the world. Virtually every vista down a street in San Francisco (population 700,000) or Seattle (population 1 million) ends in either water or hills. Even in sprawling Denver (population 1 million), the resident knows that the sprawl does not go on for ever as he looks west to see the seemingly endless snow-capped Rockies lining the horizon.

As in Britain though, the opinion-formers and movie makers live in cities where one *is* cut off from nature: New York and Los Angeles. For them, nature *is* 'out there', something altogether different from the urban world. More important for the development of the myth of the ugly city is the typical American deep yearning for the land. In their hearts, so many Americans would rather be in the big outdoors, they would prefer to be ranchers, farmers or frontiersmen than urbanites. For perhaps the majority of Americans, living in the city is not their choice, but an economic necessity; their hearts are elsewhere. With a few exceptions (most notably, New York and Chicago), the American city is not something its residents believe in, and so they are often blind to its beauty.

This, not the supposed lack of greenery in the city, is the real problem. Millions of Americans cannot believe that a built-up city can be beautiful, at least not today. I was intrigued and saddened to hear an enthusiastic New Yorker who loved her city say of Central Park, the only major piece of greenery in Manhattan, that it is 'probably the most beautiful thing in New York'. Here was the most exciting, extraordinary and alive city in the world, and yet apparently this was as nothing compared to Central Park's few trees and tired blades of grass (welcome though they are and fine though the idea of Central Park is). What about the beauty of the Manhattan skyline, of some of the skyscrapers, of the treasures in the art museums? Europeans too have something of this blindness to the beauty of the human artefacts of their cities, but not to the same degree. One cannot imagine a Londoner claiming Hyde Park to be the most beautiful thing in London, or a Parisian that the Seine is the most beautiful thing in Paris.

'Where there is no vision, the people perish.' This proverb is all too true of the decaying central areas of many cities, abandoned by the mass exodus of those seduced by the rural charms of the suburbs. The myth of the ugly town becomes reality.

Hopeful signs

So, the idea has got abroad that there is no countryside, and certainly no beauty, to be found in the typical city or large town. But there are hopeful signs that this myth is being challenged and that there are elements in the culture and history of industrial societies from which we may regain a vision of beauty in the city. I will mention a few.

For a few generations, industrial workers had lost touch with rural life themselves but had not yet entered the age of the motor car. They had to, and did, find their pleasures in the urban scene. In Britain, they are celebrated by writers such as D. H. Lawrence and Arnold Bennett. Bennett is described as having passed 'through despair and disgust into a kind of acceptance, a realization that one must look for beauty even amidst the dirt, a recognition that millions of men were going to have to make the best of living with the reality of industry. He and the characters in his books find their pleasure where they can, on canal banks, in churchyards and back streets, in municipal parks.'[5] This determination actively to seek beauty in the mundane should surely not be entirely abandoned.

There are signs that the old dogmas of recreation planning and rural planning are changing. There are no plans to extend the national parks of England and Wales, but instead local authorities have imaginatively created small country parks close to or even within conurbations. They have turned old railway lines into linear parks, and they have created adventure playgrounds. Further, the number of small nature reserves administered by the Nature Conservancy Council, often near to large centres of population, have been mushrooming.

While the 1970s saw a retreat from some of the more adventurous architecture of the post-war period, they also saw the blossoming of the factory as a fit subject for creative architecture. Some of the finest new buildings in the Britain of the 1970s are not private homes or office blocks but industrial buildings. This marks an important turn-about, not only among architects but more crucially among their clients, toward the belief that industrial production and physical beauty can go together.

I have described how the machine tends to cut us off from nature, and how this has led to a romantic search for wild nature, a search which disparages the machine. This dichotomy between sacred nature and profane machine I find profoundly sad. But many flourishing sports use tools precisely to reconnect the sportsman to nature; in dinghy racing the sail is the means by which the helmsman's body exists in delicate and exhilarating balance with the wind; in skiing the ski enables the skier to exist in balance with slope and gravity. The early French aviator Antoine de St Exupéry made a classic statement of this. In his *Wind, Sand and Stars* he wrote of his solo flights over the Sahara:

'The machine which at first blush seems a means
of isolating man from the great problems of
nature, actually plunges him more deeply into
them . . . His essential problems are set him by
the mountain, the sea, the wind.'

Clearly, though, this is not the experience of the present-day jumbo jet pilot who is almost as cocooned from nature as the factory operative. There is always the tendency for equipment to become so sophisticated that it cuts the operator off from nature, and hence for the tool to become profane.

As soon as the technical possibilities of equipment enable the sportsman to trample all over nature, success becomes virtually guaranteed and there is no sport left. So, as flying becomes too sophisticated an operation, the hang-glider bursts forth as the machine that keeps the aviator in touch with the elements. Similarly, modern firearms (or even hand grenades) would give the gamebird no chance, so the shooting fraternity insists on retaining the double barrelled shotgun: the sportsman may make technical innovations to his shotgun, but he may not replace it with a machine gun.

Improvements in climbing equipment in the 1960s led to a situation where any rock face however smooth and sheer could be ascended by means of a compressed air drill and bolts. This took all the sport out of climbing, and so the 1970s saw climbers voluntarily foregoing some of the equipment which was technically available. In a classic article, *Games Climbers Play*,[6] a leading American climber Lito Tejada-Flores describes a hierarchy of seven different kinds of climbing game, each with its own carefully devised (though totally informal) rules designed to retain uncertainty of outcome, to make success no more than a sporting possibility. Aluminium ladders are allowed for crossing crevasses in the Himalayas, but definitely not for a ten foot boulder near home!

What I find exciting about these sports is that they seem to be able to do what modern humanity generally finds so difficult: to restrain technology, to ensure that its sophistication remains at just that level which heightens rather than destroys our relation with nature. I think that these sportsmen implicitly understand what E. F. Schumacher meant when he said that small is beautiful and when he advocated *appropriate* technology.

One final source of hope is that there is a tradition in the English arts, albeit not a dominant tradition, of valuing the countryside without romanticizing or sacralizing it. The peasant poet John Clare could see beauty in a molehill or a quarry, and his literary contemporary George Crabbe, although a clergyman himself, knew well the grim struggle of the landless labourer of the early nineteenth century. A fine painting in this tradition is William Leader's *February Fill Dyke*. It shows manifest joy in the beauty of a late winter afternoon, yet the harsh reality of nineteenth-century rural life is truthfully depicted: the cottages look damp (without being ruinous and 'picturesque'), the children trudging with their firewood clearly have wet feet, and the stooping woman is obviously toiling (a fact the romantic tradition denied). A recent book in the same tradition, Rowland Parker's history of his own village *The Common Stream*, appropriately features Leader's painting on the cover.

If we can learn from this tradition to appreciate the countryside without sacralizing it, if we can learn from sports like hang-gliding and rock climbing to use technology rather than allow it to use us, if we can find insight in those factory workers and photographers who find love and beauty amidst the urban grime, then I believe there is hope for both our towns and our countryside.

We should be aiming at a society in which human beings can live whole lives at every moment and in the everyday places in which they live and work. The present division of land into profane and sacred, into places where we cannot be whole and places where we can, is disastrous for all concerned. Those who live in profane places have been abandoned aesthetically; life can be made impossible for those who live in sacred places; those who cherish the sacred live in constant fear of its profanation. At root the problem is that religious veneration has been brought to bear on physical objects and places. It is a practice our missionary Victorian forebears were all too keen to mock when they discovered it, as they thought for the first time, among the so-called primitives of the jungle.

Chapter Six

THE ENVIRONMENT AS SAVIOUR

'We were thoroughly of the opinion that if you
had good architecture the lives of people would be
improved; that architecture would improve people,
and people improve architecture until perfectibility
would descend on us like the Holy Ghost, and we
would be happy for ever after. This has not
proved to be the case.'
Philip Johnson on the International Style

In his book *The Myth of the Eternal Return*, the French student
of comparative religion, Mircea Eliade, has done us a great
service through describing the religious world-view of traditional
societies. Traditional cultures centre around myths which describe some primeval act either of the gods or of the ancestors.
The members of such societies experience their daily activities
as repetitions or imitations of these primeval acts. Only thus can
human activity be meaningful, and only thus can the individual
remain in tune with the nature of the universe. Any action which
showed originality would be literally meaningless, for the framework of ideas which makes life meaningful derives entirely from
the sacred primeval acts. This means that such societies have no
sense of progress, of history, of things changing; life consists of
an eternal return to these primeval archetypes.

This view of life is almost completely foreign to us because it
denies the existence of history. There is only one time, the
sacred time of the primeval myth, and only in this time, by ritual
participation in the myth, is there any salvation; outside of this

time lies profanity, meaninglessness. We, by contrast, tend to believe in the future; we believe things will, on balance, get better; our hope lies in the future and we have confidence in ourselves to create a better world.

In this chapter I want to explore how views of history, of that particular time – past, present or future – in which people put their hope, have affected the way they experience and mould the environment.

Classical architecture and sacred time

We will start, as in chapter three, with the Renaissance. In many ways the Renaissance provided a great boost to the modern view of history. Its new respect for the individual made it more possible for him to act out of consort with his society, and thereby it put a seal of approval on behaviour which showed originality. The new respect also shown for empirical observation, even if it contradicted accepted beliefs handed down from ancient sages like Aristotle, opened the way for modern science, and fostered the idea that human knowledge could progress.

But in painting and sculpture, and especially in architecture, the Renaissance initiated a reversion to the primitive 'archetypal' way of thinking. At the very time that Galileo, Copernicus and Newton were revolutionizing our concept of the universe, and Machiavelli, Henry VIII and Oliver Cromwell were making political innovations which were eventually to lead to modern secular democracies, while composers from Byrd to Bach were developing music in such a dynamic way that music was continually changing from one generation to the next, architects were living with an unshakeable belief in the golden age that was ancient Greece and Rome. The Renaissance's rediscovery of the intellectual and cultural riches of the ancient world led architects to abandon the Gothic style of the Middle Ages and rebuild the world in the image of a Greek or Roman temple. It was believed that the ancients understood the fundamental principles of architecture, of proportion and space, and that good architecture was that which participated in the sacred time when the Greeks and Romans articulated these principles in brick and stone.

Likewise painters believed in the Latin poet Virgil's myth – that there was once a golden age when everyone lived in a pastoral paradise. Giorgione, Claude, Titian and Poussin redrew the world as though it were a Virgillian idyll. Their style was dominant in Italy and France for three hundred years and was finally shattered only by the publicity given to the views of Malthus and Darwin about the origin of Man. Sculptors likewise recreated the human figure in the classical mould, and only in the twentieth century has this been seriously challenged.

All this started in Italy. In painting it never spread to the whole of Europe; Dutch landscape painting was hardly influenced by it at all, and English painting only during the eighteenth century, notably in the work of Joshua Reynolds. But in architecture the notion that only work which participated in the classical idiom was meaningful, spread throughout Europe and dominated Western architecture for over four hundred years. The earliest beginnings were in Florence around 1420 and the style continued, with its last fling in the impressively solid government buildings which the proud administrators of the British Empire put up throughout the world virtually up till 1914.

From Italy the classical idiom in architecture spread first to France in the seventeenth century and then to England. Here the chief proponents were Inigo Jones and then Christopher Wren, who was hugely influential through his rebuilding of London churches after the Great Fire of 1666. The eighteenth century saw the style pass over the Atlantic to influence the public buildings and dwellings of rich traders in New England. Partly through being championed by Thomas Jefferson it became the official style of the American Revolution, to be embodied in the Capitol and the White House.

The eighteenth century also saw the full flowering of classicism in Britain, in individual buildings in every market town, and on a vast and often heroic scale in many of the squares of London, Bath, and Edinburgh New Town. In Edinburgh and Glasgow while Joseph Black and James Watt were discovering the revolutionary power of steam, while Adam Smith was laying the basis of modern economics, and while David Hume was changing the face of philosophy, Robert Adam and his fellow architects were building an environment for them to live in that imitated, to the last jot and tittle of Ionic, Doric and Corinthian detail, an archetypal world of 2,000 years before. Edinburgh was dubbed 'the Athens of the North'. Bath saw the most comprehensive redevelopment that any English town has ever known. Between 1720 and 1820 virtually every building of this medieval market town was demolished and the town was rebuilt as a classical city set in a Virgillian landscape. In this primeval mythical environment the dynamic heroes of a British Empire who had spread the modern way of life to the whole world were perfectly content to while away their days of retirement. So dominant was this style that not only public buildings but the domestic dwellings of both rich and poor throughout Europe and America were built or rebuilt to re-incarnate the spirit of Athens; in fact complete communities, as in Edinburgh and Bath, were built in this image.

This comprehensiveness is what marks classicism off from all other architectural styles which have imitated the past. Chief among these others is the neo-Gothic which was a favourite idiom for the Victorians. Especially the style used for churches, it was also used for castellated houses for the rich, summer houses in their picturesque gardens, and the dwellings of artisans such as canal lock-keepers whose trades were deemed picturesque by their landlords. The neo-Gothic influence also appeared in minor features of ordinary houses, in the form of stained glass and pointed arches. But it always remained an *option* that the architect or his client could choose. Classicism was the only idiom from a past golden age that was so basic and taken for granted that for centuries throughout Europe architects had to choose *not* to use it. It is this taken-for-grantedness that makes classicism redolent of primitive religions' communal participation in primeval myths.

However, during the nineteenth century the brute facts of history were catching up with this timeless Aegean idyll. Classicism was glaringly out of tune with a manifestly changing world. Perhaps for the first time in history, nobody could avoid the realization that social change was not an accident the present generation just happened to be going through for a few years, but a process at the very heart of the human condition. Grand theories of human history became the order of the day, histories in which an inner dynamic forced human society into continual progress. The theories of Darwin, Marx, Comte, Spencer and Malthus were all the rage; they may have disagreed profoundly on many matters, but they were all agreed that man was on the move.

Maybe it was appropriate for the British Museum (built between 1823 and 1847) to look like a Greek temple, since it was chock-a-block with the contents of such temples, but surely people were beginning to see the absurdity of some other edifices. The civic celebration of Liverpool's mercantile prosperity – St George's Hall (1841–54) – was raised on its podium like the Parthenon; the celebration of Birmingham's industrial leadership – the Town Hall (1832–4) – was a copy of the Temple of Castor and Pollux in the Roman Forum.

Nineteenth-century architects – the designers of grand public buildings and the homes of the rich – were beginning to find themselves out of tune with the spirit of the age. While they were erecting classical (or Gothic) piles in stone, industrial engineers (they were not even called architects) were creating the new wonders of the world: bridges, railway stations with unprecedently vast roof spans, and crystal palaces of iron, steel and glass. Architects were being left behind and somewhere around the beginning of the twentieth century they began to wake up to the fact. No longer could they live in the mythical time of Ancient Greece. Meaning had to be found elsewhere.

At this point of crisis we must suspend the story for a while in order to explore another view of history which had an equally major effect on the environment. Then we will be able to carry the two threads on into the twentieth century.

Linear history

One of the striking features of the Jewish and Christian religions is that, from a very early time, they broke free from the primitive conception which denied history. Instead, history became the stage for divine and human action: creation, the fall of man, the historical interventions of God in human affairs (primarily in the life of Jesus Christ), and Christ's second coming. The heaven described in the Book of Revelation at the end of the Bible is portrayed as a city, something very different from a return to the garden paradise of Eden at the beginning of time. Judaism and Christianity certainly do not believe in any 'eternal return'.

In these religions, heaven is conceived not simply as a time or as a state, but also as a place. For the Jews of old, this expectation was not metaphorical but literal: in Egypt they looked forward to the promised land, and in exile in Babylon they looked for a return to that land. The whole Jewish-Christian tradition is full of a history that moves forward, and part of the goal toward which it moves is a perfect place, a promised land. It links geography to history. By providing for the landless the hope of a promised land, either actual (Judaism) or symbolic (Christianity), these religions have repeatedly appealed to the landless, to the poor and the oppressed. This hope of a future land has the potential to maintain the identity of a people who have no land of their own, as most remarkably with the Jews from AD 70 to a mere thirty years ago.

Whereas in Judaism the promised land is identified with an actual land, Israel, Christianity has tended to see the promised land as a symbol of a spiritual state. In the seventeenth century, however, especially with the puritans and other persecuted groups who left England for the Americas, the promised land came to be identified with the New World. From its very beginnings, immigrants to America have viewed that continent with a hope which is thoroughly religious.

For the puritans, their hope lay in the God who had given them the promised land as a gift. (For subsequent, more secular, generations of Americans, the hope was in the land itself, and has manifested itself since the Cold War in the belief of many Americans that their country is destined to become the saviour of the world. Hence the national disillusion in the 1970s following Vietnam, Watergate and other political faux pas; a loss of confidence comparable to the loss of faith of the religious believer.)

Sometime in the nineteenth century, the immigrants' hope underwent a subtle shift. The hope that paradise was an actual place which one could move to, became the hope that simply by moving one would find paradise. *The very process of moving*, whither it mattered not, became valued. This perhaps was the real faith of the millions of immigrants in the nineteenth and twentieth centuries, and among settled Americans today it has become transformed into the belief that the new is always better than the old. Mircea Eliade puts it like this:

'The Novelty which still fascinates Americans today is a desire with religious underpinnings. In "novelty" one hopes for a re-naissance, one seeks a new life.'[1]

This hope in a promised land, that the very process of moving will take us to a promised land, has been a dominant theme in western culture over the past 400 years and has been the hope of the millions of migrants to the colonies and the Americas who have been such a major feature of that period. Frontiers were continually expanding, new colonies being opened up.

People began to take this faith in moving for granted, and came to assume that if things got tough there would always be somewhere else they could move to where things would be better, or where they could make a fresh start. This optimism has especially characterized Americans, who occupied such a vast land; even if the first place the new immigrant settled in was not up to expectation, surely somewhere in that vast land there was a heaven on earth.

This belief took very definite shape around the myth of the great American West, where any casualties of the newly industrializing East could start again. Mid-nineteenth century America believed in the West as a kind of safety valve, drawing off any misfits from the growing conurbations of the East. Historian Henry Nash Smith[2] considers that this myth was plausible not because it was true, for those with no money or farming skills had little chance of making a living in the poorer lands of the West, but because it fitted the old image of America as the garden of the world:

'The doctrine of the safety valve was an
imaginative construction which masked poverty
and industrial strife with the pleasing suggestion
that a beneficent nature stronger than any human
agency, the ancient resource of Americans, the
power that had made the country rich and great,
would solve the new problems of industrialism.'

People believed more than this. They saw the frontier not simply
as a sump which would drain all the bad fluid from industrial
America, but as a positive influence for good that shaped the
American character. Frederick Jackson Turner stated this in a
classic article in 1893, *The Significance of the Frontier in American
History*. Jackson believed that the frontier stripped the
European immigrant down to the savagery demanded by bare
survival, and then 'little by little he transforms the wilderness,
but the outcome is not the old Europe . . . The fact is, that here
is a new product that is American.' More effusive still, he wrote:

'To the frontier the American intellect owes its
striking characteristics. The coarseness and
strength combined with acuteness and
inquisitiveness; that practical, inventive turn of
mind, quick to find expedients; that masterful
grasp of material things, lacking in the artistic but
powerful to effect great ends; that restless,
nervous energy; that dominant individualism,
working for good and for evil, and withal that
buoyancy and exuberance which comes with
freedom.'[3]

That is to say, the frontier was not only the promised land, but
it also made new men and women; it redeemed them from
savagery and from their European ways (there was some debate
as to which was worse) and made them anew. The wilderness
and the life of the frontier truly had the power to save people.
The fact that Turner was speaking for millions is amply demonstrated by the way in which Americans today still play at being

frontiersmen, by the dreams of many American men to own a ranch out West, and by the fact that in the national mind the good old virtues of family life and integrity are located somewhere on a farm in the mid-west. Indeed, the worldwide popularity of the Boy Scouts and their faith that camping creates character suggests that Turner was articulating a faith held not only by Americans.

Whatever the truth or falsity of this myth, Turner also pointed to an unpleasant fact: there was no longer a frontier. From 1880, he reckoned, there was no more land available. The empty West was no more. But Americans continued to believe in the promised land. Increasingly California came to bear this mantle[4] and in the last few years it has been transferred to the newly-popular sunbelt of Arizona and New Mexico. With miniaturization and computerization, proximity of industry and population to raw materials is becoming less and less important, and industry is more and more able to be sited in those ideal places where people want to live.

There was a further legacy of the frontier mentality which people did not really become aware of in any numbers until the 1960s and 70s. This was the American's attitude that the place where he lived was disposable. If you fouled up your nest, no matter, for you could always move some place else. This disposability of the landscape, once it became apparent, was perhaps what really disgusted and motivated the environmental movements which America has spawned since the early 60s. American writer J. B. Jackson[5] has argued that the typical American mid-western rural landscape was created in the nineteenth century by evangelical settlers who, with their otherwordly attitude, took too little care of the soil. When the soil became exhausted, they would move on with blithe optimism that God had another land waiting for them. In his view, Christians have been influenced not so much by God's injunction in Genesis for man to 'fill the earth and subdue it'[6], as by the belief that *this* world is of little importance.

Anyway, by the end of the nineteenth century there was a crisis in the optimistic hope of a promised land. The crisis derived partly from the fact that the period of expansion in which

Europe exploded into all the world, roughly AD 1500–1900, was historically very unusual in that new land was continuously available and at the same time the modern mind was in the process of being formed. The result was that this state of never-ending expansion was considered normal rather than a historical anomaly, and it has taken mankind, and particularly Americans, rather a long time to face up to the reality.[7] Over the generations we have become too used to believing that when things get tough there is somewhere else we can up and move to, where things will be much better and we can make a fresh start. Geography, a new environment, had been the solution for human ills for four centuries, and had become such an ingrained response that it was not easily shed.

The modern movement in architecture

We may now draw our two threads together. By the 1880s both the classical idiom and the faith in the frontier had reached the end of their respective centuries' long paths. It was no longer believable that a brand new virgin environment existed out there where we could leave all our mistakes behind and solve all our problems; we really had to face up to them ourselves in the present environment. There was no escape. At the same time, people could no longer call on the image of Athens to inject meaning and beauty into the places where they had to live and from which there was no escape.

This then was the crisis and the challenge that was facing architecture at the turn of the twentieth century. On the one hand, much more was being demanded of it than ever before. People had begun to realise that there was no alternative to creating for themselves an environment (even the city) which was beautiful, livable-in, functional and comfortable; they could no longer rely on the use-once-and-throw-away environment of the frontiersman or emigrant.

On the other hand, the classical idiom which architects had employed for four centuries was no longer plausible. There seemed no alternative but to take the industrial beast of iron and steel by the horns and tame him into the service of architecture for everyman. It was in rebuilding Chicago following the great fire of 1871 that, for the first time architects pressed into service the materials of iron, steel and glass which had hitherto been employed only in engineering works; it was here in the 1880s that the steel-framed, high rise office block was pioneered.

It is significant, I think, that the closing of the frontier and the beginnings of modern architecture coincided almost to the year. For, with no bolt-hole left, fame and fortune had to be sought *here*, not elsewhere, and it became doubly imperative that every conceivable resource be used to make *here* into as good an environment as possible. Modern architecture began to replace the promised land as the repository for people's hope. The hope was still, note, in a new environment; what had changed was where it would be and who was going to create it.

Louis Henry Sullivan, chief of the new Chicago architects said: 'With me, architecture is not an art, but a religion, and that religion is but a part of democracy.' Why did architects link their new-found religious calling with democracy? The reason is that up till then their clients had been the rich. As it has been said, in the Victorian era the rich had architecture and the poor had slums. What was acutely embarrassing about the architects' humiliation at the hands of the technically superior achievements of the engineers was that the engineers' structures – railway stations, factories, bridges and so on – were for the use of the whole community. Architecture had been shown up not only as technically backward but also as socially elitist. So, many younger architects set themselves the mission of creating a better world not just for the rich but for everybody. Architecture would have that power to save people which previously the frontier had had. Good architecture and good planning would produce good people. In the 1920s this utopian faith in architecture became a powerful force not only in the USA but also throughout Europe. Its great high priest was the Swiss architect nicknamed Le Corbusier, who produced imaginative plans for building complete cities, plans which look now like science fiction. The movement was christened the 'International Style' in 1932 by Philip Johnson, who recalled recently (rather ruefully):

'We were thoroughly of the opinion that if you

had good architecture the lives of people would be
improved; that architecture would improve people,
and people improve architecture until perfectibility
would descend on us like the Holy Ghost, and we
would be happy for ever after.'

It is perhaps difficult to comprehend now the confidence with
which this hope was held. This was no wishful thinking; it was
hope in the sense that the apostle Paul used the word – a
conviction of things which are to come.

One of the dogmas of this new faith was *reason*, and nothing
epitomizes this more than the glass-walled skyscraper. This was
pioneered in the 1920s by the German Mies van der Rohe, and
the spirit behind his thinking has been described by Robert
Hughes in his television series *The Shock of the New*:

'Straight lines, clear thought and extreme
refinement of proportion, detail and material.
They were acts of faith, absolute and austere. But
he loved the idea of crystalline building, the pure
prism. So his designs in the Twenties believed in
salvation through glass architecture – and his
belief was almost religious.'

Le Corbusier described the house as 'a machine for living in'.
The age of science had really come to the front door of everyman, who could no longer conceive of his home as a haven from
the world of science, technology and industry. For Le Corbusier,
salvation was to be found by embracing science and technology,
not by running away from it.

In the 1920s at a German school of architecture named the
Bauhaus this view was systematically propounded, and since
then it has influenced the whole of the design profession. The
Bauhaus' contention was that every artefact, teapot as well as
house, should be scientifically designed before going into mass
production. Their first manifesto stated clearly their aim of a
new heaven on earth:

'Let us create a new guild of craftsmen, without the class distinctions which raise an arrogant barrier between craftsmen and artists. Together let us conceive and build the new structure of the future, which will embrace architecture and painting and sculpture in one unity and will rise one day towards heaven like the crystal symbol of the new faith.'

The new faith was first articulated in England through the garden city movement, spearheaded by Ebenezer Howard and Patrick Geddes. It arose out of the typically English tradition of romantic socialism with its vision of the happy egalitarian community living in balance with its rural surroundings. The early experiments at Letchworth and Welwyn Garden City were pragmatic and therefore more successful that the typically Germanic idealism of the Bauhaus and of Mies; although Howard and his successors were most certainly utopian in vision, they had the pragmatic political skills necessary to make their vision into a workable reality.

Only after 1945, however, did the modern movement, the garden city and the fully planned new town, really become politically acceptable in Europe. The Second World War, which had devastated property in the way that the 1914–18 war had destroyed lives, left the governments of Europe with the task of rebuilding a continent. The destruction was so complete in some cities that a total solution had to be found; the desire for a new order was expressed in Britain in the landslide victory of Labour in the 1945 General Election, so for the first time there was the political will as well as the physical need for solutions on a Le Corbusian scale. And so began the saga of high-rise in Britain – the attempt to embody German idealism and American panache in more subdued vein in an English field. The attempt largely failed, if we are to believe the current move away from high rise flats. So, too, began the attempt to embody Fabian socialism in the form of new towns. And this largely succeeded, if one is to go by the students of planning who come from all over the world to study them.

In other countries, the dream of the perfect planned city underlay the foundation of brand new capital cities – Canberra in Australia, New Delhi in India, and later and most spectacularly Brasilia in South America. With the eyes of the nation, indeed of the world, upon them, planners and architects wanted to show what could be done given a virgin site and no millstones from the past hanging around their necks. They attempted to express through civic architecture a whole national identity and all the values of modernity that the politicians of these nations wanted to prove they shared. Brasilia is the only truly Corbusian city ever built.

Faith in rebuilding the environment followed a different time scale in the USA. The States did not suffer the destruction of the Second World War but in the early 1960s, with signs of unrest among the nation's urban blacks, politicians realised that they would actively have to woo the urban black vote. And so came President Lyndon Johnson's War on Poverty. Results had to be got within the space of four years or so, before the next presidential election; optimism was politically necessary in this situation and it was considerably more optimistic to believe that the problem lay in the poor environment that the blacks inhabited rather than in any genetic inferiority. So a massive programme of environmental improvement was initiated.

But sad to say, utopia did not arrive (which is not to say the genetic explanation was correct). A mere four years after the start of the War on Poverty, American cities were literally burning because of the rage of many blacks. At the same time, the new tower blocks in Britain were being condemned for their inhumanity – they cut people off from one another, isolated housewives, were dangerous for children, and were a target for vandalism. They had been built on the premise that houses were machines; but machines have no place for the human individual, for community, or for neighbourhood. Designers like Le Corbusier had attempted to eradicate the unpredictable and the disorganized; they had wanted to make cities into safe, undemanding places, which could be totally planned in advance, like a production plant. There was no place for the client to make his voice heard. Any parts (= people) of the machine which were out of step with the overall plan, or any parts in conflict with each other, would defeat the whole purpose of the machine. So, the new architecture did not make nicer people, in fact quite the reverse.

Once again, we had placed an almost religious faith in physical objects and in the environment, this time architect-designed buildings, slum clearance and planned towns. And not surprisingly, this faith proved to be ill-founded. Since the late 1960s, this has produced a new crisis for planners and architects. 'Client participation' is now all the rage, and is clearly a gesture of repentance from the professionals for having so ignored the human beings who have to live in the houses and cities the professionals design. But the utopian hope has gone; architects are left with the mundane task of building houses for people, not heaven on earth. Which is probably what they should have been doing all along.

Where, though, has the hope in the redeemed environment gone? Chiefly into the ecology movement. Stridently declaiming the technocratic arrogance that led industrial mankind to trample all over the environment, political ecology has taken over from modern architecture the convinced hope that restructuring our relation to the physical environment will bring us salvation. Like modernist architects, indeed even like the industrial rapists of the earth they so deplore, political ecologists believe in reason, science and human knowledge as the keys to a redeemed world. Only this time the knowledge is called 'ecology'. Faith in technology remains too, this time in 'appropriate technology' rather than big technology.

Others, though, have abandoned faith in the redeemed environment. As the War on Poverty stuttered, the psychologist Jensen suddenly caught the imagination of intellectual society in America. He claimed that IQ differences between blacks and whites were due to genetics rather than poor environment; the answer was not to be found in the environment after all. Others retreated inwards, to a beautiful internal landscape created by LSD. Sociologists Laurie Taylor and Stanley Cohen in their book *Escape Attempts* describe this as a shift from landscaping to mindscaping.

The escapism of others is more conventional and still latched onto escape to an actual place. For them heaven on earth is to be found for two weeks a year on whatever magical island happens to be in vogue with the tour operators – and the further it is removed from the unredeemed city environment back home, the better. Pop songs have been full of imagery of a physical escape to a place where true love can flourish. For the Seekers it was their *Island of Dreams*, while for the Beatles in their *Octopus Garden* 'we would be warm, below the storm, in our little hideaway beneath the waves'.

The terror of history

One of the most fashionable responses has been to re-locate heaven from the immediate future back to the past. At the beginning of the chapter, I contrasted our awareness of history with traditional societies' denial of history. Such societies do indeed have a terror of history, for to believe that human affairs were subject to change would be to invalidate their archetypes and myths; life would literally become meaningless. We could never recapture this experience of a static world for we know in our bones that things *do* change.

So what of those today who would like to retreat to a golden age, who have a terror of history and of the mess that we moderns have made of it? As moderns, they are aware of change, but like primitives they wish to deny it. They attempt to invent a past golden age, but these attempts inevitably involve myths which, unlike the myths of traditional societies, are inappropriate. Inappropriate because the myths can make no more than a semblance of sense of the history and change that are inescapable. No one golden age is entirely convincing, and so golden ages proliferate as the search for the (non-existent) perfect age goes on. Rather than a coherent specific archetypal time when our ancestors and the universe were at one, all there can be is a diffuse nostalgia for the past.

These myths frequently contain images of the landscape, buildings and artefacts of the past. The past is even less tangible than the present and requires correspondingly more expression in material forms to make it real. Television is an excellent medium for conveying nostalgia precisely because it can dwell on the visible manifestations of the past and so make the past real and almost graspable. Britain's *All Creatures Great and Small* and America's *The Waltons* are classic examples: the long lingering shots of rural Yorkshire and of the Walton's homestead are what provide the nostalgia. The characters we know are modern actors pretending to be of another age; the landscape and the farmhouse, though, seem indisputable.

The novelist Margaret Drabble points to another reason for the importance of landscape in nostalgia, when she says that 'landscape represents at once the changing and the unchanging'. Buildings and landscapes change more slowly than people, than economic booms and slumps, than governments and most social institutions; and when landscapes and buildings do change, the change is clear-cut, not fuzzy as with people. It may be difficult to trace how Harold Wilson or Richard Nixon subtly changed during their periods of political office, but to identify change or stability in buildings and in landscape is simple: it is writ large. By picking the right landscapes, you can surround yourself with an image of just the amount of change you find acceptable.

Photographs play a particularly important part in the task of creating nostalgia through landscape. As an animal or a type of building nears extinction, so photographs of it multiply; the photographs reassure us that it still exists. Still photographs, as contrasted to movies, freeze time and thereby give the subject the appearance of stability. (This is particularly true of the picture postcard and other photographs taken on bright sunny days, for they give the impression that this is how the subject 'really' is and looks. It is not true of good photographs taken in stormy weather, for they imply that change is imminent; one cannot believe that the subject always looks like that).

Old photographs, though, highlight change. On seeing an old photograph of a familiar place (or face) what we notice first are the things which have changed and only then do we see continuities. The photograph thus clarifies further what a building or landscape has already clarified: it shows unmistakably what has changed and what has not changed.

Nostalgia is almost always a wish for a past which is out of reach. The recent past threatens to drag us back into it. Something can be romanticized only if it is already dead. Red Indians were not romanticized so long as they posed a real physical threat to white Americans, and nature was not romanticized until we felt we had mastered her. As Shakespeare put it, 'He's good, being gone'. Likewise, no historical period is romanticized until it is dead and gone; then it becomes inaccessible, and comforting illusions about it can be fostered without fear of contradiction. Long past history shares with nature the honours for being the prime subjects for illusory myth making, for neither nature nor the dead will contradict the mythmaker.

While nostalgia requires a past which is firmly in the grave, it also requires a past which is relatively recent. We have to be able to imagine that we could have lived in it, that if only things had been different, that past might still have been with us today. One can feel a wistfulness that one was not born a couple of generations earlier, one can feel a wistfulness for the 1920s, but however much one *admires* the Elizabethan era or Ancient Greece, one can hardly feel *wistful* for them.

So the prime candidate for nostalgia is that period which is only *just* out of our reach, but within the memory of our grandfathers. Which is why the top rating TV series *The Waltons* and *All Creatures Great and Small* both depict the 1930s, and why, in the late 1970s, the 1930s came into vogue among cultural connoisseurs and why the exhibition on 'The Thirties' at the Hayward Gallery in London was so popular. This nostalgia for the 30s is very different from the interest generated by the historical novel or play, in which the audience explores another era, its good sides and its bad sides, and comes to some independent judgement about the era. Rather, whatever hardships the Waltons face, their era and what they represent is *essentially* to be preferred to the present; the viewer has no freedom to decide otherwise. He is invited to escape for an hour or so to a golden age – even more golden in the case of James Herriot than the Waltons.

Falsifying the present

But one thing such programmes do have in their favour: they *do* make clear that, however much the viewer may wish otherwise, we do not actually live in the 30s. This is not so with some other manifestations of nostalgia, which reconstruct the landscape of the present in the image of the past. The *Artists' Britain* calendar is a good example. It contains reproductions of paintings by some of the most popular contemporary landscape artists, such as Rowland Hilder. The calendar may be taken as a fair cross-section of how successful contemporary painters see the landscape of Britain and how many millions of their countrymen who buy reproductions of their works like to see it. There are several things to note about these paintings:

First, their subject matter consists almost wholly of small market towns, the countryside and seascapes. Large towns, especially industrial ones, simply do not exist. The 1981 calendar was unusual in containing three large cities as locations, but their treatment is most revealing. *May Morning Near Nottingham* by Sir John Arnesby Brown is a vista from rising ground over the city, a style of painting which, as I mentioned earlier, went out of fashion a century ago. The foreground is very rural, as are the hills in the far distance which puts smoky, dirty Nottingham firmly in its place: it is an island of muck in an otherwise beautiful, rural land. As if to drive the point home, the foreground field is being ploughed by a white shire horse! Can this really be Nottingham in 1981? This is certainly no celebration of the city!

Then there is London, in *Royal Naval College, Greenwich* by Anthony Flemming. The view across the river is from the exact point Canaletto painted his *Royal Hospital at Greenwich* some 300 years ago, and again the style is archaic. At first glimpse one might even confuse the one painting for the other. However, on inspection there are significant differences. Whereas Canaletto flanked the hospital with miscellaneous buildings, Flemming has it in a pristinely green setting; whereas Canaletto has real contemporary ships sailing past the hospital, Flemming puts in some old Thames sailing barges, probably more of them than still exist in the whole world let alone this particular hundred yard stretch of water; whereas Canaletto's figures are a cross section of his society from boatmen to lords and ladies, goodness only knows who the figures in Flemming's barques are supposed to be. Canaletto was one of the finest recorders and celebrators of the urban scene, which throws into relief Flemming's essentially anti-urban vision. Canaletto loved to record the contemporary scene; Flemming wants to see the present as though it were the past.

The third 'urban' picture, *The Tall Ships Gather, Mill Bay Dock* by Alan Simpson, is hardly an everyday scene, with several tall ships and one old steamer. Of the vaguely slummy-looking buildings overlooking the dock, only one is painted in any detail and it has pretty Georgian sash windows with all glazing bars intact.

This brings us to the second feature of all the *Artists' Britain* paintings: they omit almost all signs of the present, in particular any sign that we live in an industrial society. The image is of Britain as it was pre-1914, yet it masquerades as the present. In the 1981 calendar, there are paintings of market day in two small towns; there are no cars, only a couple of pick-ups clearly belonging to stall holders; no no-parking lines, no traffic signs, nothing to tell us this is 1981.

Other paintings do show modern sailing dinghies, yet these are primarily leisure craft which are themselves pre-industrial in ethos if not in materials. Transportation is always by horse: *Ratley, Warwickshire* by S. R. Bodmin has a horse and cart in the foreground waiting for a man to open a farmyard gate; *Burford, Oxfordshire* has the empty main street covered in thick snow with a man leading a horse and trap up the hill. (I have never seen this particular tourist Mecca free from parked cars by the score.) There are coal-fired tramp steamships (pre-1914), and one phone box introduced to provide some red in an English landscape which often exasperates the artist by its lack of that colour. In the 1981 calendar of thirteen paintings, this exhausts *all* the contemporary artifacts: one phone box, a few sailing dinghies and four pick-up trucks. This is the world English people would like to imagine they inhabit; this is nostalgia at its most dishonest, and landscape is a powerful tool in such dishonesty. Paint *people* dressed up in 1913 clothes and people would just laugh at you; paint the landscape in 1913 cleverly enough garbed and it is convincing.

Perhaps the fact that these paintings are reproduced in a *calendar* is significant; the message is surely that, even as the days roll by one by one, nothing really changes. Calendar photographs of countryside, mountains, flowers, and natural wonders all say the same thing.

Of course, no-one has to look at such reproductions or buy calendars. But young children have little option in the books and television programmes made specially for them. And here one usually finds just the same dishonesty. The Britain that is portrayed is small town and village Britain, of around 1930 (an advance of a few years on *Artists' Britain*, but then children are younger so one can be more adventurous!). There are cars and buses, but not modern ones. There are bakers' shops and butchers' shops but no supermarkets. This is the Britain that fictional villages like Trumpton, Chigley and Camberwick Green conjure up. Of course there are brave exceptions, but significantly one feels that in these instances the artist or producer has consciously had to resist relapsing into the mythical style and strive to portray contemporary townscape truthfully.

This rustic sentimentality is not a purely English phenomenon. The most popular American landscape painter of the 1970s has been Andrew Wyeth, whose work also depicts rural life of a generation or two ago. Wyeth does have the merit of being a far better painter than his English counterparts and, as with them, I suspect it is not so much the painter as his admirers who are sentimental for the past. Wyeth is doubtless portraying quite faithfully the archaicly rural pieces of Pennsylvania and Maine that he lives in. He paints what he sees around him; the purchasers of reproductions of his work obviously do not like what they see around them in Levittown.

Back to nature

Perhaps the most popular way of escaping history and its terrors is to escape back to nature. If the calendar on one's wall represents the 1920s, if a visit to a stately home represents the age of Queen Elizabeth I, then a trip to the wilds represents pre-history. The wilderness, the high hills, the sea are all primeval; they take us out of human history altogether. If there ever was a golden age, surely it was before homo sapiens came onto the earth and started mucking around with it.

This has always been the appeal of nature. This was why the children of Israel found the nature gods of neighbouring peoples, the gods who confirmed the regularity of the universe through the regular passing of the seasons, far easier to live with than the one Lord God who was to be discovered not in immutable nature but in the very changeability of history.

Evolution and ecological balance are two chief ways in which today we understand our relationship to the natural world. And both deny history. Both postulate that there is a basic underlying principle to all life which unites human beings to the whole universe. Evolutionary theory locates mankind within the archetypal process of evolution, and either denies the significance of human history or proposes that human history is simply an extension of this immutable process. Ecology would abolish history if it could, preferring human beings to exist in the time-less idyll of an ecological balance with all other species.

In fact, not just evolution and ecology, but natural science as a whole is perhaps the nearest thing that modern societies have to the *cosmos* of history-denying primitive societies. In primitive thinking, the human world reflects the very structures of the universe, which cannot change, and this is just how modern science views man. In playing the role of the scientist, one temporarily absents oneself from history. A morning at the lab immersed in the timeless structures of the universe is even better than fifty minutes' immersion in the world of James Herriot or the Waltons.

Early scientists like Newton believed that the laws of the universe were given and sustained by God, and that this God could intervene and change them as easily as he could intervene in human affairs and human history. For Newton, science was no escape from history. But modern science believes that its discoveries about the universe are ultimate and immutable; and thereby the modern scientist takes his leave of history. Which is perhaps why the natural sciences are regaining the popularity among students which they lost in the heady days of the late 1960s when young people believed they could change the world.

Chapter Seven

HOUSEWIVES ALL

'He will satisfy his desire for security by creating a
place belonging to him.'
Jacques Ellul, The Meaning of the City

So far, I have tried to document the continuing, if often unre-
cognized, existence of religion in contemporary society and its
effect on our dealings with the environment. One of the functions of religion is that it provides fixed points which enable
people to maintain their bearings. (Whether these bearings are
correct depends largely on the truth or falsity of the religion in
question. I myself would not altogether trust bearings based on
the doctrine of progress or on the worship of the individual).
Religion enables people to feel at home in the universe; to feel
that there is a structure to things, and that they have a part in
it.

This is necessary because without religion or some kind of
faith mankind is, metaphorically speaking, homeless. As a
species we are biologically unique in that very little of our
behaviour and perception is governed by instinct, and consequently a member of our species needs to *learn* so much in order
to survive. Even those activities based on instinct, such as sleep,
sex, eating and drinking, also involve a great deal of social
learning: it is through culture that we learn when and what is
the proper occasion for these activities, and what is their *meaning*. So much so, that a hypothetical human being who relied on
his instinctual programming and was not *taught* by peers and
parents would not be able to exist as a human being. Consider

the 'wolf-children' occasionally found in India and elsewhere, and their inability to function in society. Our biological equipment leaves us like nervous children on the first day at school, utterly lost and in need of direction. Homeless. Adrift.

This inadequacy comes precisely from the fact that we are thinking beings, homo *sapiens*. We are able to reflect upon our situation, wanting to know what things *mean*, and instinct provides us with no answer to such questions. We need to *know*, to know who we are, where we fit in, where we are going. Even the most primitive of peoples create myths to answer these questions. Instinct provides no answers to such questions; it leaves us homeless.

Ecologically, as well as biologically, we are in a peculiar position. Members of all other species automatically slot into a niche in their local ecosystem, determined by the particular combination of other species in that system. But man the tool maker, homo *faber*, has some choice in the matter. What ecological niche I will adopt will depend to a large extent on myself: on whether I am a tender of sheep, a grower of corn, or a smelter of iron. Human communities find themselves in an enormous variety of ecological niches. Ecologically speaking, we are homeless, looking for a place to rest our heads.

Judaism and Christianity also teach that in a sense human beings are, or rather have become, spiritually homeless. This is symbolized by the story of Cain and Abel in which Cain, having murdered his brother, cut himself off from his creator. As a result he loses his bearings, and the story describes him as a fugitive and wanderer on the earth, living in the land of Nowhere. Cain responds to this intolerable situation by creating a home of his own, independent of God; he builds a city and a family.

Biology, ecology and theology all point in the same direction: that human beings are by nature homeless, but are also incorrigible home-makers, trying to ensure that they do not remain homeless for long; making sure, indeed, that most of their members never come to recognize their homelessness at all.

Home-making is largely a cultural affair. In my book *A Long Way From Home* I described at length how human culture (that is, the 'way of life' a society possesses, not the 'high culture' of arts and letters) provides us with a home in the universe. It provides us with the knowledge that we have a place in the scheme of things, however undesirable (in the case of slaves, for example) that place may be.

But human cultures are fragile. Many Britons and Americans at the present time feel that their way of life is under threat from various quarters, that their way of life is vulnerable. The cultures of the Aztecs and Tahitians demonstrate how astonishingly quickly human societies can collapse; European gunpowder, alcohol and avarice were the simple instruments which destroyed cultures that had existed, apparently stably, for centuries or millennia.

As well as being frail, human cultures are intangible, so they need to be *materialized*. They need to be made visible and tangible in goods and chattels, houses and tools. All the artefacts of a people reflect their culture back to them and makes it definite and real. All their artefacts, together with the land they have moulded and made their own, make up a people's environment. They inhabit a physical world which confirms their cultural world.

The process of making culture tangible is necessary, if only for the sake of young children. They have much to learn even before they have mastered language. How do they do it? Mainly by exploring their physical environment. From the breast come warmth, fullness and contentment and thence the concept of being loved; from touching and handling forbidden objects (for example, touching a hot stove, or eating earth) comes the concept of law-breaking; from the contents of their bedrooms (frilly lace and dolls for girls; toy cars and balls for boys) comes the concept of what it means to be a boy or a girl. Thomas Aquinas was surely right when he said that, with human beings, intelligibles are derived from sensibles.

It would be most disorienting for the child if the physical environment he was exploring and the way of life he was learning did not fit together. (To repeat an example from chapter three, it is doubtful that a child could take on board a strong sense of privacy if rooms did not have doors). It is no less important for adults that their culture and their physical surroundings should reflect and reinforce one another.

When this does not occur, people no longer feel at home in their environment. For example, in the USA since the 1960s many people have been painfully aware of the contradiction between their optimistic faith in Man and in Progress, a faith few questioned, and the mess that their environment was becoming. Very distressing for a people who believed themselves to be the epitome of human progress. The result was a mutual challenge. The belief in the inherent goodness and wisdom of human beings challenged the fact of urban dereliction, which came to be defined as pollution and is now in process of being cleaned up. And the physical dereliction (along with other 'anomalies' such as Vietnam and Watergate) challenged the belief in the perfectibility of the human (and particularly the American) race, resulting in a sharp decline in utopianism and a profound lack of national self-confidence.

Such contradictions between a people's way of life and their environment simply highlight what is the dominant trend: that human beings try to make their physical setting in the image of their cultural setting. Take private gardens, for example. Americans are typically *expansive* – in their personalities, their economy, their personal generosity, and also in their gardens. The major feature of the American garden is the expanse of lawn, unbounded by hedge or fence; basic and spacious, like the American personality. The English garden, by contrast, is much more refined, with its delicate flower beds in which every detail is in its right place. This reflects English culture which rests on fine class distinctions, much more structured than the open society of the United States. Australian and New Zealand suburban gardens are more schizophrenic. Some follow the English pattern of structured order, to the point where 'mowing the lawns' has become a national fetish (as for some Americans). Others, most notably the increasingly popular 'native' gardens, are free and natural, with minimal intrusion into the original habitat. The two approaches represent corresponding diametrically opposed trends in antipodean society: a pulling towards and a drawing away from its English origins, both culturally and politically. This mirroring of culture in horticulture is rarely deliberate; it is just that people like a garden that meshes with their way of life, and they would not want a garden that did not. Many Americans, for example, find the English garden over-refined and fussy, like English culture; many English find the American garden lacking in refinement, like American culture.

In other places, the landscape has been deliberately contrived to embody the values of its creators. Certainly this was true of the eighteenth-century landscape gardeners; it is true of professional designers and architects, whose task it is to ensure that a product or building meets the goals and aspirations of the client; and it is true of professional planners, whose task it is (in theory) to ensure that any changes to the environment are in line with the democratically expressed wishes of the people.

Arranging the world

This striving to create a unity between our way of life and our physical environment, between human beings and the world, ultimately between Man and Nature, expresses itself at two levels. First, there is the way we human beings conceive of our environment in our mind's eye; second, there is the way we physically arrange our environment.

First, the mind's eye. A common but incorrect view of perception is that the eye (or the ear or nose) receives a jumble of sensations from the outside world which is fed into the brain which then decides what this jumble means. The brain is thought of as a scientist, producing hypotheses out of vast accumulations of data.

Actually it seems that collecting sensations and imparting meaning to them cannot be neatly kept apart like this. It seems that the ordering of the sensations into a coherent pattern comes at the very earliest stage of perception. The gazelle does not run away because it has seen a splurge of yellow light which it decides represents a charging lion which it decides represents danger. Rather by a process of instinct and learned associations it *sees* danger. Likewise, if I blindfold you and give you objects to handle and ask you to describe what you feel, then unless you have been specially trained you will not actually describe physical sensations but will say 'this feels like a stone', 'this is metal'. Perception operates through very broad categories – like 'stone' and 'metal'.

Nor does perception consist simply in overlooking the uninteresting parts of the visual field and focusing on the interesting parts. Sure, when I'm waiting for the bus and it eventually comes into view, I see the bus rather than the brass bell-pull of the house next to the bus stop or the cirrocumulus clouds in the sky. But the point is that when I *do* select something for attention, it is riddled through and through with meaning. The bus is late, or full; or its arrival means I'll get to the shops before they close.

In a sense Aquinas' dictum that we apprehend intelligibles through sensibles can be turned on its head: we also apprehend sensibles through intelligibles. Both these statements highlight different facets of the same process: on the one hand we learn morally charged concepts through our dealings with the physical environment, on the other hand we perceive that very environment through morally charged concepts. The point is that there is a constant striving to unite the two into a coherent system.

So, in the very process of perception we begin to accommodate the physical environment to our own pre-formed concepts and categories. The physical world is seen in the image of human concepts and purposes.

An example of this may be found in the perception of mountains.[1] Before people had any desire to climb them, mountains were seen largely as barriers; certainly the Alps, straddling Europe, were a highly inconvenient barrier. The word 'mountain' referred to the lump that got in your way. For example, 'Mont Cervin' was the name of the high mass between the Swiss village of Zermatt and the Italian village of Breuil; its focus was the lowest traversible point, which we now call not a mountain but the 'Theodule *Pass*'. Today, when we now look at that whole mass, what *we* see as expressing its mountain-ness is not its lowest point but its highest, the 'Matterhorn' (German for 'Mont Cervin'). Two hundred years ago, this point was merely mentioned in passing as 'L'aiguille du Mont Cervin' (the sharp point on Mont Cervin). *Then* the height of this mountain mass was 3,300 metres, the height you had to climb to cross it; *now* it is 4,400 metres, the height you have to climb to get to the highest point.

When in the late eighteenth century people began to climb the mountains of the French Alps in order to get to the top, a completely new language was formed. Odd bumps and pimples and depressions in the terrain which formerly had not attracted attention became vital in the work of discovering a passable route to the summit and then informing others of this route.

These features – cirque, coulouir, arête, gendarme, col, and so on – became the definitive shape of the mountain; the mountain came to be perceived as *composed* of these features, and their origin as linguistic symbols to aid mountaineers became forgotten. Originating as more-or-less useful human concepts, they soon became objective features of the mountain; they became things rather than concepts. An arête (a ridge), once a means to a human end, became a feature of the natural world. Human purposes and the mountain itself had, in the mind's eye, become indistinguishable.

I mention mountains because the invention of a new way of perceiving them was unusually rapid and deliberate and so the human-centredness of environmental perception was made unusually clear. But the intertwining of human purposes and needs with what the eye actually sees is by no means limited to mountains. Residents of cities invent a simple mental map of their city not only for the sake of getting about the place but also so that they can feel at home in it. The resident reduces the chaos of thousands of higgledy-piggledy streets and houses into a coherent order, and the more he can simplify it the better he feels. In his important book on environmental perception *The Image of the City*, Kevin Lynch says

'A good environment gives its possessor an important sense of emotional security. He can establish an harmonious relationship between himself and the outside world.'

That is, we need to feel at home in our environment.

Establishing a harmonious relationship between oneself and the outside world is something scientists as well as city residents do. Over the last four hundred years there has been a remarkable parallel between the way scientists have viewed the natural world and the way people have experienced their own society. To give four examples:

Early scientists such as Newton saw nature as given by God and upheld by Him much as social institutions were.

More 'enlightened' scientists of the eighteenth century dispensed with God as 'an unnecessary hypothesis' and saw the natural world as operating according to its own internal laws; at much the same time revolutionary philosophers were beginning to see society in the same light.

Darwin's theory of evolution through the survival of the fittest was developed in parallel with the ruthless laissez-faire capitalism of nineteenth-century England and with various social theories which justified this in the name of progress. These ideologies of social evolution and Darwin's theory reinforced each other to create a coherent view of both the natural and the human world.

As industrial society has become more and more complex, the view has emerged that the basis of everything is not elements, particles or objects, but relationships. So Einstein's theory of relativity and ecology's emphasis on the relationships between species have both emerged in the century which is pre-occupied with social and human relationships.

In citing these examples, I do not claim, as some rather crude sociology has done, that scientists simply project into the natural world the sort of relationships they experience in society. If anything, the opposite is true: we use impersonal concepts from science to understand human relationships.

In a fascinating article *African Traditional Thought and Western Science*[2] the anthropologist Robin Horton has explored the circumstances which affect which way round the process works. Horton is interested in explanations: how human beings explain things. And he is particularly interested in comparing the way modern western science explains things with how traditional African thought does. Explanations work by finding unity and order in apparently diverse things, by revealing simplicity in what appears complex, regularity in what appears as diverse. They reduce chaos to order. Frequently analogies are drawn from familiar things to explain the unfamiliar.

In agricultural African societies nature is by no means completely tamed and always threatens drought or some other disaster. By contrast, personal relationships are rather stable and predictable. So regularity, familiarity and order are found in the personal, and are used to explain the diversity and unpredictability of the impersonal world of things. Illness is explained not in terms of germs and molecules but in terms of personal relationships: perhaps the sick person has had a curse placed on him. Poor harvests are explained not by pests and climate, but by the community having offended the spirits.

In the modern world, however, the reverse is the case. As Horton says, 'In complex, rapidly-changing industrial societies, the human scene is in flux. Order, regularity, predictability simplicity, all these seem lamentably absent. It is in the world of inanimate things that such qualities are most readily seen. This is why many people can find themselves less at home with their fellow men than with things. And this too is why the mind in quest of explanatory analogies turns most readily to the inanimate.' So we explain the personal in impersonal terms such as drives, forces and energy. Whereas the African explains that a person is sick as a result of offending his neighbour, we reverse the explanation and say that the social offender is 'sick'. This use of the impersonal to describe the personal has contributed to the depersonalization which so many deplore but seem powerless to prevent.

There is, of course, a powerful residue of traditional thinking in modern society. Along with the great Old Testament sufferer, Job, and the people whom Jesus healed, we still want to find personal, moral explanations for human illness and suffering. 'Why me?' cries the mother of the deformed baby; 'Why him?' cry the prematurely bereaved. Physical death and physical handicap would somehow be more manageable if there were a moral, personal explanation.

Whether the personal is used to explain the impersonal, or

the other way round, we all do strive to produce a coherence between the two, between our values and the natural world, between culture and our physical environment.

This striving towards coherence is not simply a mental process of eye and brain, it shows itself too in our actual physical dealings with the environment.

Of course when we build houses, factories, and bridges or remake part of our environment in any way, on one level we are clearly performing a straightforward physical task for a straightforward purpose. We build houses because we want to keep out the rain, we build factories because we want to manufacture a product, and we build bridges because we want to cross a river.

But at another level we are performing a symbolic act of reordering our world. The manufacturer who transforms a raw material into a finished product, or the cook who transforms a raw leg of lamb into a cordon bleu dish, is restructuring the physical world from something *raw* – rough, unrefined, unfit as it stands for human purposes – into something of *value* to human beings. The physical environment is being remoulded so that it becomes a part of, and valuable to, our way of life. Meaning is being injected into material that was previously meaningless. One spruce among the thousands in an unknown forest is transformed into the bedroom door which protects my privacy; a few tons of iron ore in an unknown mountain become the motor car which announces my social status to the neighbours.

In money economies, this addition of meaning and value to a raw material is generally reflected in an increase in the price tag attached to the material. Economics has become the discipline which more or less monopolizes the study of this process. But this increase in the material's economic value generally occurs only because the material has received increased significance and meaning for people, and it is this underlying process which I now want to look at. Through the study of societies which do not use money, most notably Claude Levi-Strauss' study *The Raw and the Cooked*, it has become clear that the production of goods from raw materials is at root to do with the injection of meaning, rather than of £s or $s, into a material; the £s and the $s are simply the index we use in modern societies to measure this. If a product did not have significance and meaning for the buyer he would not want it and it would have no economic value. (Of course, a few prestige goods have meaning *because* they are expensive, but this is the exception that proves the rule.)

I would like to explore this by looking briefly at three very ordinary ways in which we reshape the contemporary everyday environment: house-building, housework, and gardening.

House-building

Marx and Engels expressed a common modern belief when they asserted the primacy of physical survival:

'Life involves before everything else eating and
drinking, a habitation, clothing and many other
things. The first historical act is thus the
production of the means to satisfy these needs, the
production of material life itself. And indeed this
is . . . a fundamental condition of all history.'[3]

A plausible enough supposition, but those who have had more time and resources than Marx and Engels to explore ancient and primitive human cultures have generally come to the opposite conclusion. Architectural historian Amos Rapoport in his book *House Form and Culture* has surveyed ordinary domestic dwellings throughout the world and has concluded that even in the harshest times, building a house involves a symbolic as well as a physical re-ordering of the world. He says:

'If provision of shelter is the passive function of
the house, then its positive purpose is the creation
of an environment best suited to the way of life of
a people.'

And Lord Raglan in his *The Temple and the House* says:

'Given a certain climate, the availability of certain
materials, and the constraints and capabilities of a
given level of technology, what finally decides the
form of a dwelling, and moulds the spaces and
their relationships, is the vision that people have
of the ideal life.'

In modern societies, it is ideals such as privacy which ultimately
explain the shape and form of the typical house. Towns-people's
ideals about the value of rural life explain the location of millions
of homes in the suburbs. The value placed on personal mobility
explains the prominent position of the garage in many new
houses. It also helps to explain why it is so popular to convert
old mews stables in London into fashionable dwellings; no matter that these were where the servants and horses used to live,
their merit today is that, with the garage occupying the whole
of the ground floor, they provide a physical expression of the
centrality of the motor car in modern life. In primitive societies,
the house embodies the very structure of the universe; the hearth
or the smoke-hole in the roof are considered to be one with the
mythical centre of the world.[4]

Le Corbusier attempted to rid the house of symbolic meaning
and reduce it to its physical function as 'a machine to live in'.
The fact that he failed highlights the impossibility of purging the
domestic dwelling of all symbolism. For Corbusier's view of the
house as a machine was itself a manifestation of a technological
culture and its dehumanized conception of humankind. So even
in his work, house and culture together create a symbolic universe, unified by the worship of reason, technology and human
knowledge.

Housework

Maintaining houses involves upholding, or reforming, the symbolic meanings that went into the building of them, and the
main way this is done is through the day-to-day activity of
housework. The housewife's enemy is *chaos*, and her never-
ending task is the continual rescuing of order from the disorder
produced by energetic toddlers, untidy teenagers and thought-

less husbands. For the housewife the house is no 'machine for living in', but the universe in microcosm of which she is guardian. The house, despite the destructive tendencies of its other inhabitants, must continue to display and embody the family social order as interpreted by the housewife. She has standards which, although invented by herself, she projects outside herself and believes to be obligations which she must conform to at all costs.

A crucial part of this operation is the identification and elimination of *dirt*. As anthropologist Mary Douglas says in her book *Purity and Danger*, although dirt is experienced as something physical, what makes it dirt is not physical at all. A particle of earth in the garden is not dirt, but the same particle in a toddler's mouth or on the living room carpet is. Dirt, like pollution, is matter in the wrong place. Dirt is essentially disorder. And housework, the elimination of dirt, is the continual restoration of order, of things to their right place.

The housewife is thus the landscaper of the home environment, ensuring that it reflects back to its inhabitants their values and way of life. She is doing with her house what all human beings are doing the whole time with their environment, and so she typifies the whole environment/humankind relationship.

I have already suggested that the importance of this task of unifying culture and environment is indicated by the disarray caused when the two fall out with each other. We take it for granted that they should reflect one another, and often only notice when they fail to do this. This helps account for sociologist Anne Oakley's initially amazing finding that, of the forty typical housewives she interviewed, twenty-four said their husbands commented only negatively, never appreciatively, about the results of the wife's housework, and *none* of the wives found their work rewarded by spontaneous appreciation.[5] Those who keep environment harmonious with culture are taken for granted exactly because we take it for granted that culture and environment should be harmonious. The low status of the housewife (and for that matter of the local authority town planner) derives precisely from the importance of their work. Sustaining the taken-for-grantedness of the everyday world is crucial to human well-being, yet the near invisibility of such work means that we do not reward it highly.

Even sophisticated academics share this denigration of the housewife's role, as the following quote in an otherwise excellent article by sociologists Colin Bell and Howard Newby clearly shows:

'The really vital decisions about the nature of a woman's 'place' – such as the location or whether to sell it, as opposed to the colour of the wallpaper – are taken by husbands not wives.'[6]

Now clearly the location of a house is an important decision which greatly affects the lives of husbands, wives and children, but surely decisions such as the colour of the wallpaper are hardly unimportant. Whether one is surrounded by fine floral prints or mallards taking off from a garish pink background is a vital means of representing oneself both to oneself and to others. I could live in a house located virtually anywhere because I could always claim I had little choice in the matter; but I could never live in a house with mallards taking off from every wall because that *would* say something about me.

Gardening

Gardening also illustrates several aspects of how we like to transform the physical environment into a 'cosmos' replete with human meaning. As in housework, there is the constant struggle against chaos, except that here it is weeds rather than dirt which represent chaos. Weeds are like dirt in that they cannot be adequately defined physically: a dandelion is a pretty flower in a meadow but a weed in a herbaceous border. Weeds are plants out of place; flowers are plants in place. Weeds are plants which are not properly controlled by the gardener. They are disorder, and gardening is the creation of order.

Gardening has the peculiar attraction of creating an environment which is manifestly responsive to the efforts of the gardener. The trouble with housework is that the house all too often displays not the work of the housewife but the destructive activities of the children. In the garden, though, there are no other humans working against the gardener, only the birds, the neighbour's cat and the weather, so he has the satisfaction of working with the raw materials of nature to create an order that is his very own.

Although the weather or the birds can indeed be a thorn in the flesh, he actually enjoys this contact with nature. This is because the nature that the gardener encounters is Mother Nature, the fertility goddess. He may curse at the gale that blows down his runner beans, but this is not nature red in tooth and claw. This is no brutal struggle for survival since unlike the professional farmer or subsistence peasant who has to make a living out of the soil, the gardener can never be financially ruined or reduced to starvation by the weather.

Gardening involves making and experiencing an environment which is responsive to the human order and which is smiled on by benign Mother Nature. It is a world in which human beings and the universe are one. It is perhaps not insignificant that for millennia in Western history the garden has been a symbol of paradise.

In conclusion, whether in the mind's eye or in their physical manipulation of the world, human beings attempt to create a universe which is unified. This is what the ancient Greeks called the *cosmos*: a unified totality containing heaven and earth and all living things, gods and humans. We attempt to create a human home which contains all that is and which is therefore self-contained and manageable. Not only the Greeks, but most cultures have constructed a cosmos of this kind.

Judaism and Christianity are a major exception, for central to both is a God who is outside the cosmos. Although Judaism and then Christianity (notably in the writings of Paul) took over the word *cosmos* from the Greeks, they have always been careful to distinguish the creator God from his created universe. This is probably the main reason for the unpopularity of radical Christianity which refuses to allow God to be co-opted by humans as part of their cosmos. This was also why the ancient Israelites were always attracted by the religions of their neighbouring races. Their God was uncomfortable. Being outside of the created cosmos he could exercise radical criticism from the outside of human beings and their world. So the co-option of the Jewish-Christian God for human purposes is a travesty of these religions; and it is something people have been doing for millennia.

To build a city which excludes God (like Cain's) is one way of producing a world totally under human control. To build a civilization and then co-opt God into it, as has been done in much of what has passed for Christianity, is another. To have a human home which is open to the judgement of a transcendent God is altogether inconvenient; one does not feel at all at home in such a world. Not unless one worships this God, and that would entail the loss of the cherished illusion of human autonomy over the universe.

In the next three chapters I want to look at some of the ways in which cultures have attempted to create a cosmos. First to be considered will be the question, 'How have they decided to relate to the natural world?' The medievals faced the problem of fitting the natural world in with a Christendom dominated by the Christian God; later centuries had to decide what to do with a Christian God who refused to become part of a natural world which appeared increasingly to be all that existed.

Chapter Eight

AT HOME WITH NATURE

'Nature is perhaps the most complex word in the
language.'

Raymond Williams, Keywords

Human beings are the only creatures adaptable enough to be
able to live on virtually any part of the land surface of the globe.
We have no unique ecological home on the earth, no fixed way
of relating to other creatures. This makes our relation with the
natural world a peculiarly open-ended thing. On the one hand,
storms, volcanoes and the like can make the natural world seem
all powerful and fit only for reverence and awe; on the other
hand, we seem to be able to tame vast amounts of it and bring
it under our control. And where does God fit into this? Is he to
be found in the awe of earthquake, within the human mind, or
outside of the universe altogether?

Thinking about the nature of the natural world and the place
of man and God has been a perennial occupation of all known
human societies. The answers produced have not merely been
of academic interest, but have profoundly affected both culture
and landscape.

Many books have been written on the nature of the natural
world, and still more on how earlier times and other societies
have conceived of it. In this brief chapter I can do no more than
sketch a few of the major approaches which have informed
western civilization; my aim is simply to show that, without
some resolution of the Man/Nature/God question, there can be
no feeling at home in the world.

Three basic approaches have influenced western history: those that centre all things around God (theocentric views such as the Jewish and medieval views), those that centre all things around human existence (anthropocentric views, such as those propagated in the Renaissance and in the industrial revolution), and those that centre all things around the natural world (such as romanticism and scientism).

The Jewish view.

In the Old Testament view, the earth, the heavens above, all things have been created by God. People are allowed to use the earth, indeed they are commanded 'to fill the earth and subdue it; and have dominion over the fish of the sea and over the birds of the air and over every living thing that moves upon the earth' (Genesis 1.28). Human beings are given authority within creation, but as always in the Bible this authority granted by God does not imply that we are free to do as we like; rather, the authority is delegated by God, we are responsible to God and may have our authority removed if we are irresponsible. Of course, many people have used the commission in Genesis to justify unlimited, greedy and man-centred exploitation of the environment. In just the same way many of the kings of Israel took their God-given political authority to mean they could do as they liked. The prophetic books interpret their abuse of authority as the cause of political disaster for the nation of Israel, and in just the same way misuse of the land leads to the nation's exile from the land.

The Old Testament view of land – like that of many African tribes – is that it cannot be owned. The people are its caretaker, its steward. This belief was embodied in the law of 'jubilee', a legal institute which decreed that every fifty years land had to be returned to its original owners, so preventing the accumulation of property by the few. Whether the jubilee was ever actually carried out is not recorded, but it nevertheless highlights the Hebraic view that land is a gift from God.

This view is also embodied in the historical fact that on entering the promised land – a land flowing with milk and honey – the Children of Israel took possession of a land which was already complete with cities and vineyards and fig trees. However hard this may have been on the unfortunate Canaanites who had lived there before and had put their labour into creating this abundant land, the theological significance for the Israelites is clear: land is not something people have to strive for and in which they may feel smug, secure and proud. Land is a gift from God – the God who had provided them with food from heaven (in the form of manna and quails) when they were homeless in the wilderness of Sinai.

For the Israelites, land is held not for as long as the people have an adequate defence force and practise good horticulture, but for as long as they keep faith with its Giver. The way to be at home in the creation is to relate properly to its creator. Thus the covenant relationship which is the main subject of the Old Testament is between God, the people and the land. If the people keep faith with God, they may stay in the land. This may be contrasted with the usual Christian view today – of a covenant between God and *individuals*. This latter view means that Christians have great difficulty in seeing how politics, economics, ecology and so on fit in with their faith. The ancient Israelites had no such difficulty, for politics, economics and ecology – embodied in the concept of the land – were a central part of the covenant.

Although the people of Israel have this covenant with the creator, they are very firmly placed within creation. The crucial distinction in the Hebrew scriptures is not Man/Nature, but the Creator/Creation. Indeed the concept of nature, meaning the material world other than man, does not exist there. Rather, the view that all creatures are on the same level is very strong in the psalms, in which mountains, waves, rocks and so on, along with human beings, are described as created by God, and together worship him and manifest his glory. So man's dominion over the earth need not give him airs.

Nor does creation have meaning in and of itself. The creation may be diverse, wonderful, awe-inspiring and powerful, but the awe felt in the presence of a storm causes the Hebrew to worship not the power of the storm itself but the creator who controls such power. To take one psalm among dozens:

'The floods have lifted up, O Lord,
  the floods have lifted up their voice,
  the floods lift up their roaring.
Mightier than the thunders of many waters,
  mightier than the waves of the sea,
  the Lord on high is mighty!'

                         Psalm 93

So the Hebrews considered there were two entities of very different sorts, the creator and his creation, with clear relationships between and among them:

CREATOR (God) | CREATION (Man, mountains, seas, the heavens, animals, all living things)

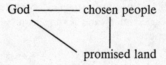

The Middle Ages: God and Nature

The Christian Middle Ages were heavily influenced by the biblical view of creation, though the crucial element of 'the land' did not really feature in the Christian view, since Christianity had emerged as a distinctly landless sect within the Roman Empire. By the Middle Ages, the covenant looked more like:

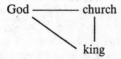

Christian thinking was also heavily influenced by the Roman concept of 'nature'. The Latin word *natura* originally referred to the essence or quality of a thing, and later came to be used in a wider sense as the nature of things in general, *natura rerum*. Some writers shortened this phrase back to *natura*, which is the word the medievals inherited. By the fourteenth century this nature of things had taken on more substance; it was thought of as the force which directs the world.

So this idea of 'nature' was Latin in origin. It had nothing to do with the Hebraic biblical view; it existed in its own right. How it related to the Christian God was therefore problematic. Raymond Williams describes the medieval problem and its solution:

'Nature herself is at one extreme a literal goddess, a universal directing power, and at another extreme an amorphous but still all-powerful creative and shaping force . . . There is then great complexity when this kind of singular religious or mythical abstraction has to co-exist, as it were, with another singular, all-powerful force, namely a monotheistic God. It was orthodox in medieval European belief to use both singular absolutes but to define God as primary and Nature as his minister or deputy.'[1]

This solution in terms of *God/Nature* is crucially different from the Hebraic *Creator/Creation*, for Nature is virtually on a par with God. It is really only her deference to traditional religion which prompts her to be content with being God's deputy rather than a challenger to his supremacy. She is, in fact, a lesser deity herself. It was an uneasy truce which was not to last for long.

The increasing importance given to nature in the God/Nature formula may be seen in late medieval oil paintings.[2] In early medieval art, there was little attempt to represent the natural world as we see it, in perspective. Painting was not meant as representation at all, but as symbolism of spiritual truth, 'the world of grace'. Colours such as gold, blue and red had well-known symbolic meanings, and many pictures used simple coloured backgrounds to inform the spectator of what the picture meant. But from the thirteenth century artists began to explore the technique of perspective; they were taking more seriously what their eyes as well as what their soul told them.

The increasing importance of nature over grace is perhaps best shown, however, in the subjects depicted in paintings. In early medieval art, the natural world is of virtually no importance as a subject. Artists chose religious subjects – saints, miracles performed by Jesus, the crucifixion and so on. Grace rather than nature was what really mattered in the (officially) unworldly life of the medieval church, and art reflected this. However, in the fourteenth century, in the background behind these religious subjects painters began to include landscapes, often with no thematic connection to the main subject. The Virgin Mary was still holding the baby Jesus, but behind peeped a Tuscany landscape. Not only was there no thematic connection between the two, but neither was there any connection in terms of visual perspective. Mary would be seated on a high-backed gold throne which physically cut her off from the landscape. Other common ways of separating the foreground of 'grace' from the background of 'nature' were to locate Mary in a room with the landscape viewed through the window, or to put her in a garden with the landscape beyond a wall. Artists did not know how to integrate nature and grace, any more than theologians did.

The Renaissance: Man and Nature

Early Renaissance painting destroyed the uneasy balance between the two autonomous forces of nature and God. The physical barrier between Mary or Jesus and the landscape vanished, and they simply became ordinary human figures set in a landscape. Nature became the framework within which scenes of grace were enacted.

This created the problem of how to impart religious meaning to these ordinary figures. No longer could a gold or blue curtain be set behind them. Mary could be given significance by making her especially beautiful, but this invited the danger of making her a kind of Venus to be gawped at. Haloes were safer, but they appeared increasingly odd, for real people in real landscapes do not ordinarily go around with circles of light on their heads. Effectively, nature had triumphed at the expense of grace.

Not only this; the religious life itself had become humanized.

The sacred figures of medieval painting were now simply human figures in a landscape. The free human spirit of Renaissance man had replaced the medieval religious soul as the driving force behind arts and letters; the splendid new works of Florentine princes and merchants – political, economic and architectural – were becoming as important to them as the state of their spiritual soul. The ambition of a man was to be remembered by his peers for his earthly works rather than by Saint Peter at the gates of heaven for his spiritual grace.

The medieval problem was a tension between an autonomous nature and a monotheistic God. This was now replaced by a new tension: between the newly emergent free human spirit and nature which was year by year claiming more ground. How was human civilization to relate to the goddess Nature, autonomous Man to autonomous Nature?

The response to this problem was related to the ascendancy of the merchants and their capitalist orientation to material things. Nature became something to be appropriated, possessed. Fifteenth-century Florence witnessed a rebirth of the old Roman taste for having a country villa to complement one's town house. The wealthy burgher would now enjoy the countryside by possessing his own little piece of it. Soon trade was expanding throughout the world, and it was not long before colonization became the only way to guarantee the continued existence of the new lands as sources of raw materials and as trading partners. Land was no longer a gift, but something to be grasped.

In due course, the idea of possession came to be applied to one's own body as well as to the land. The Christian idea is that one is responsible before God for one's body (this is the basis of Christian sexual morality). In its place came the idea that the autonomous individual owned his own body. Of course, this applied only to the male. The woman's body was owned by her husband (or worse, by her employer or landlord). The women's movement of recent years is challenging this, but not, note, the idea of ownership; indeed the basis of its challenge is that the woman owns her own body. In this view, equality between the sexes is conceived of as equality between capitalist proprietors.

The idea of ownership of one's body is the basis not only of capitalist sexual relations, but also of capitalist economics. For it means that the individual owns the labour that his or her body is capable of, and is therefore free to sell this labour on the open market. Direction of labour by the state or some other authority is abhorrent for the same reason as is sexual abuse by another: both entail the loss of proprietorial rights over one's own body.

The desire to possess was manifested in the tradition of western oil painting which sprang from the Renaissance. I have already mentioned how this new form of art depicted the world as experienced by the eye, and so centred the world around the individual. The subjects of paintings, especially religious subjects, no longer existed in their own right; their reality now became dependent on the human observer, and any subject which was not portrayed as it appeared to the human eye increasingly came to be seen as unreal. The human eye came to possess the world, in that, without it, the world did not exist. The world's reality no longer derived from having been created by God (something which the ingenious symbolism of medieval art had expressed), but from being perceived by human beings.

Oil painting focuses on the solidity and texture of the paint surface, and so it was eminently suited to making the world appear tangible and graspable. This possessiveness could be made real with some subjects more easily than others, however. In the western tradition of the nude, for example, the female body was increasingly portrayed as an object to be possessed through being looked at. Landscape was more difficult. Certainly, many landscape paintings commissioned by wealthy landowners to depict their holdings portray land as an object of possession, and this idea underlies many a vista painted from rising ground. But the problem with landscape painting is that two key components are sky and distance, both of which are intangible, incapable of being turned into a thing which can be grasped. In fact the sky is often seen as a symbol of freedom, exactly because it is the one thing which cannot be grasped and possessed; indeed it is not actually experienced as a 'thing'. But since the sky did not have the quality of 'thing-ness', and since painting had eschewed ethereal symbolism, how could the sky be painted in oils? This was a major problem for landscape painters for centuries, and it is probably significant that the first school to dare to paint pure landscapes and seascapes which were not simply a background to some event of human interest were seventeenth-century Dutchmen living by and large in poverty. They did not own land themselves, nor were they sponsored to paint landscapes since patrons were not interested in the subject. So these artists were not trying to possess their subjects and were consequently able to attempt to paint sky and light as it really appeared to them. The results were paintings which had little appeal to buyers because they did not exude the quality of possessiveness. Bourgeois art connoisseurs of the time were more interested in interiors, a gold vase among the fruit of a still life, portraits, and other such manifestations of their solid wealth and industrious character.

The Renaissance ideal of relating to the natural world through possession reached a climax in eighteenth-century England. It was embodied in the country house and its landscaped park which, through possession, united civilization at its most refined with nature at her most beautiful.

One feature which helped produce this semblance of unity was the 'ha-ha'. The typical country house had formal lawns immediately in front of it, with the more informally-landscaped park, kept cropped by grazing animals, beyond. The problem was how to prevent the grazing animals and their destructive hooves encroaching on the formal lawns. Building a wall would have destroyed the effect, for it would have symbolized a barrier between natural beauty and the civilized life. The solution was the ha-ha, a ditch with a retaining wall about three feet high facing the park which formed a barrier to the animals but remained invisible to the house.

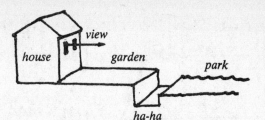

The view from the house was uninterrupted, and the whole world became a garden, tractable to the ordering propensities of the rational human mind. In so far as the garden was a symbol for paradise, the whole world became paradise. The creation of such vistas became known not as landscaping but as landscape *gardening*; the entire landscape was contrived to appear part of the garden.

Even more sophisticated than the country house and park was the attempt to inject the Renaissance ideal into urban locations. In Bath in the 1760s John Wood the younger completed the Royal Crescent, a grand and palatial shallow crescent containing thirty town houses and facing a landscaped park behind which trees were later planted to hide any further urban developments beyond. Here was architecture as urbane as any in the world, yet the outlook for its residents was entirely rural. Civilization (Man) + landscape (Nature) = the cultivated life. This sophisticated architecture-cum-landscape was all the more remarkable for being the property not of one wealthy person but of thirty; in being imported from country to city, the ideal was also being extended from landowning aristocrats and gentry to the new burgeoning middle classes. The building of what is actually a row or 'terrace' of houses in a crescent rather than a straight line was a crucial innovation for adapting the ideal to urban purposes; the amount of landscaped land a crescent requires in order to form a rural outlook for all the residents is much less than the amount required for a straight terrace. So the crescent enabled the Man/Nature ideal to be realized in an urban setting where land was scarce, and where some dozens of households wanted to enjoy the same view.

The Royal Crescent was built on rising ground which had the advantage of creating a vista over the land falling away below. This was symbolically important because it reminded the spectator of those oil paintings made from rising ground, a style which had the connotation of possession, even if, in the case of the Royal Crescent, none of the land visible was actually owned by the residents. The ground in front of the Royal Crescent also contains a ha-ha, which aids the residents' illusion of their territory stretching as far as the eye can see.

In the ensuing seventy years, the crescent was repeated in many fashionable British cities. Nash's Regency crescents facing Regent's Park in London are a straightforward continuation of the theme of creating in an urban setting the appearance of the country house and park. Others, such as Bath's Lansdown and Camden Crescents and Bristol's Royal York Crescent, are built on virtual precipices so that the view looks straight over the city to the hills beyond. The steep ground acts like the ha-ha, giving the impression that the city and countryside beyond lie within the domains of the crescent's residents.

Steep land which gave this kind of view allowed another building innovation. If the rural view was the extensive countryside beyond the city limits, it was no longer in short supply, and this obviated one of the main reasons for building crescents. So in the nineteenth century the building of town houses on precipices ceased to rely on the crescent; straight rows, reverse crescents (that is with the convex side facing downhill), and indeed any plan that the land dictated, became common. Examples may be found in the backs of those terraces and circuses (circles) in Edinburgh New Town which overlook the ravine of the Water of Leith stream and beyond to the Firth of Forth and the Fife hills; similarly in Glasgow's Park Terrace overlooking the Kelvin Gardens and the Clyde to the hills beyond.

Likewise, the crescent was not required for the fashionable seafront terraces which sprang up when the seaside became popular in the early nineteenth century. The view was free, and all the developers and speculators had to do was to cram as many hotels and boarding houses as possible onto the seafront.

Landscaping on this grand scale attained a balance between urbane living and country views which worked for the relatively few landed gentry and for the bourgeoisie of the early industrial revolution. It also worked for a rather greater number of people so long as they restricted their enjoyment of it to a brief holiday at the seaside. But the ideal was so powerful that more and more of the middle classes wanted it. At the same time, the bourgeois ideals of privacy and private ownership were becoming stronger, and people did not want to share their view with others. So the terraced town house was replaced by the large 'semi' of the 1840s (in which only two households occupied the same building) and then by the detached villa of the late nineteenth century. The detached house was best of all, as it could be surrounded by a natural landscape all its own – the private garden. At the same time, the expansion of the industrial core of the city, together with its lower-class residential accretions, were taking over the once-rural view of the more elevated Georgian and Regency crescents and terraces. The shipyards of Govan became the view from Park Terrace. So those in search of a balanced relationship between urbanity and rurality had to retreat to the newly fashionable suburbs where fresh air and fields were still in abundance. By the 1930s this process had become so unstoppable that there were cries that the entire rural hinterland of big cities was becoming devastated by urban sprawl.

By this time, the Renaissance balance between urbane architecture and the rural paradise had clearly been lost forever. The trouble had been that this ideal was fundamentally undemocratic; it could work for the few, but not for the many. Not every house can command a vista. The ideal was a product of the enlightened western mind, but it could not survive those other products of enlightenment – democracy and an ever-expanding middle class.

As the Renaissance ideal of a balance between man and nature broke down, not only in architecture but also in other areas, it split into two threads which for the last 200 years have existed side by side. On the one hand there was the ideal of civilization triumphing over nature; on the other, there were various scientific, philosophical and romantic movements which tended to see reality as composed of nothing but the natural world. These two strands form our next three sections.

Industrial Revolution: domination over nature

Although the old land-owning aristocracy saw themselves as the sole and rightful owners of their land, this was generally tempered by a strong sense of responsibility – to God, to their heirs, and to their employees. The landowner saw himself as the one to whom the management of both his land, and in the wider sense *the* land (meaning the nation), had been entrusted. Only his social class was competent to manage it, which is why he would be against democracy (this form of paternalism is still found in South Africa today). This sense of responsible management, together with the assured belief that one's land would never go out of the hands of one's children and grandchildren, meant that possession of the land did not warrant unbridled exploitation of it. For the landowner, possession meant ownership in trust. The relationship with the land was ownership/responsibility, a halfway house between the Old Testament concept of stewardship/responsibility and the modern capitalist concept of ownership/irresponsibility.

Not so, however, for the rising bourgeoisie. They were the *nouveaux riches*, who had not inherited wealth from generations past but had, they believed, won it by their own enterprise. Land for them was not gift but achievement. For the old landed gentry, landholding was something received from past generations and held in trust for future generations, but for the bourgeoisie land and wealth were to be enjoyed and displayed in the present. Material goods were the symbol of a status which would otherwise have no recognition. Like the husband who is not sure of his wife, possession becomes possessiveness.

Moreover, the new power and technology provided by the industrial revolution made possible the illusion that this possessiveness was without limits. This sense of man's triumph over the natural world came to be shared by capitalist and socialist alike; certainly the Marxist vision of utopia assumes it. Thanks to new technology the idea of history as never-ending progress was able to blossom out from a trendy idea held by eighteenth-century intellectuals to an ideology held out to the masses and, some of the time, believed by them. The railway steam engine, puffing through meadow and city alike, was an altogether *visible* symbol that progress was being made. Belching and bellowing, it was power made manifest. (This is in contrast to many of the technological breakthroughs of today, which often lie behind the surface: few of us have *seen* a silicon chip, a DNA molecule or a space-ship. Even the power of a modern diesel or electric locomotive is hidden away). As historian Leo Marx puts it, 'the awe and reverence once reserved for the Deity and later bestowed upon the visible landscape is directed toward technology or, rather, the technological conquest of matter.'[3]

In the concept of 'conquest' there is certainly no idea of a balance between civilization and nature. The idea of conquest was extended to all relationships with the natural world, not just industrial operations. For example, it was the dominant idea behind *The Times* special supplement in July 1953 celebrating the first ascent of Mount Everest. The leading article is entitled: 'The Long Supremacy of Peak XV' and continues:

'A mountain must be climbed because it exists. A symbol of the supremacy of Nature, it must be added to man's collection of souvenirs by which he measures his progress in the fight against the oldest and most primeval enemy . . . Everest stood inviolate and indifferent, awaiting attack, and the longer it waited the more omnipotent seemed its power . . .'

Note here not only the language of conquest but also the term 'progress' and the idea of 'Nature' with a capital 'N' as the enemy. The conquest language continues (my emphases):

'Everest is a peak surrounded by peaks; each
attempt to scale it must therefore be considered in
the light of a *military campaign*. In addition, Everest
is protected by the weather, so that there are only
two periods of the year during which *an assault*
can reasonably be launched . . . Seen in retrospect
therefore, the campaign against Everest has been
a thirty years' *war*; *skirmish* has followed skirmish,
and each has contributed to the intelligence upon
which the next has based its *attack*.'

So, the conquest language of a triumphantly industrial society is the means by which an essentially playful and decidedly non-utilitarian sport is purveyed to the excited millions. The climbers themselves, and even the reporters who accompanied the expedition and whose reports make up the fine print in the rest of the supplement, did not use the language of conquest; but this merely serves to highlight the fact that what people wanted was not to hear what it was really like but to have confirmed the myth of the conquest of Technological Man over the poor Virgin Nature.

The sexual imagery here is significant. Human beings are portrayed as active, dominant '*man*', while nature is a passive *female* who can do little to avert the inevitable conquest. Given that the human relationship to the environment in industrial society is conceived as an essentially male activity, it is interesting to ask how women in that society relate to the environment. I have already referred to research which has highlighted the differences between the ways boys and girls are encouraged to interact with their environment. The boys go out and explore and conquer. The girls stay at home; their activity is confined to making corn dollies out of corn which men have reaped or knit with wool from sheep which men have sheared.

This may have some bearing on something I have noticed in

the course of country walks with various companions. Male companions tend to be interested in the *distance*: they scrutinize the map in order to name a mountain or a river which has just come into view, as though they are assessing whether the mountain may be scaled or the river forded, either today or at some future date. Female companions are more interested in the *foreground*: they stop to admire a flower here, and to name a bird in the hedgerow there. The men's approach to their environment seems to be implicitly active, naming the mountain so that they can climb it; the ladies are passive, classifying and admiring species for the pure joy of it, without any intent to transform this aesthetic exercise into physical domination. Perhaps the difference may be summed up in the observation that women love naming animals, while men love shooting them; and in the nineteenth century, the ladies sketched the hills, while the gentlemen climbed them.

Because the ideal of mankind dominating nature so completely tilted the scales on one side, it is not surprising that there have been equally determined attempts to tilt them the other way. I will not discuss these at any length, because I have already given them considerable space, especially in chapter two.

Romanticism: domination by nature

Sometimes the romantic ideal was held by completely different people from those who believed themselves the masters of nature; certainly Wordsworth was no industrialist. But many hundreds of thousands of people have worn the hat of man-the-conqueror while at work, and the hat of the romantic-overawed-in-the-presence-of-nature during their vacations. A professional guide who provided adventure holidays for executives in Canada's Hudson Bay country at the beginning of the century described them:

'I have seen them come from the cities down
below, worried and sick at heart, and have
watched them change under the stimulus of
wilderness living into happy carefree, joyous men,

to whom the successful taking of a trout or the
running of a rapid meant far more than the rise
and fall of stocks and bonds.'[4]

Doubtless on return home they soon changed back again, as
have many more since then. The contradiction between these
two lifestyles need not bother them, however, for together they
can create a kind of schizoid personal balance. It is a bizarre
way to create a feeling of 'at home-ness' in the world, but it is
effective nevertheless. Certainly the two ideals create a schizoid
landscape, with sacred preserved wildernesses on the one hand
and ruthless profane urban scapes on the other.

Scientism: nature as everything

I have already mentioned the way evolution and ecology are
sometimes called upon as a total framework for understanding
and directing human activity. In such a view, science becomes
the basis for morals, because the natural world science investi-
gates is the only world there is. This involves a shift from *science*
(the systematic observation of and theorizing about the natural
world – one form of valid knowledge among many), to *scientism*
(the assertion that science is the *only* form of valid knowledge).
In philosophical terms, this is logical positivism, the belief that
all statements which are not empirically verifiable, or at least
falsifiable, are meaningless.

This view makes nature even more pre-eminent than romanticism does, for it allows no possibility at all of stepping outside
of the natural world. Nature has eased out not only God, but
humanity (as commonly understood) too. As a way of feeling
at home in the universe, it brings with it many problems (for
example, the annihilation of love, responsibility and freedom)
which have frequently been pointed out by its critics. But it does
have the attraction of daring. It is a bold solution to the old
question: how to relate God, Man and Nature. Its answer?
Simply abolish first God and then Man. Whether people can
live with such boldness is another matter; and that is what will
determine whether or not scientism will enable them to feel at
home in the universe.

Chapter Nine
SIGHTSEEING

'They say the world is a beautiful place – we'll
have to go there sometime.'

Humorous postcard, 1972

One way of trying to feel more at home in the world is to
explore it, to see how other peoples live, to gaze at the wonders
of the world. In the last two decades tourism has emerged as
one of the world's biggest and fastest growing industries. Why
is it such big business? Why do the Japanese, Germans,
Americans and Dutch tour the world looking at each other's
countries?

Something rather different is going on here than in the New
Yorker's traditional annual vacation in the Maine woods, the
Manchester factory worker's annual trip to Blackpool, or the
southern Australian's search for a winter suntan on the Gold
Coast. In the traditional vacation, the aim is to sit on the beach,
to camp in the forest, to fish, or to wander along the prom;
basically to stay in one place, and perhaps return to the same
place year after year. A contrast is sought from one's normal
existence which will provide a refreshing break. This is recreation – re-creation of an inner soul which has been tattered by
fifty weeks in the factory, office or kitchen.

The tourism that will be discussed in this chapter has its roots
not in the static seaside or lakeside holiday, but in the grand
tour that the ladies and gentleman of Northern Europe used to
make around the cultural treasures of Italy. It is tourism in the
sense of touring the world, and its aim is re-creation not of the

self but of the world. One need not actually go around the world, nor even leave one's home country, to engage in this kind of tourism; all that is necessary is that one makes a tour to see places.

Much of the behaviour of the modern tourist may be explained in terms of a dilemma. On the one hand he wants to take hold of the world and explore it; on the other hand he daren't look too closely, in case something disturbing turns up which serves only to confuse. So, the task of the tour operator, the hotelier or the tourist guide is to give the tourist *the impression* of having grasped, understood and appreciated the place of interest, but to guarantee to protect him from any unpleasant experience. The tourist may be allowed to be mildly surprised, but he must never be disturbed or challenged. Given the diversity of cultures in the world, and of the values held dear by different cultures, there is indeed much that could shock and disturb the visitor were he really to look closely and take the people and places seriously.

It is this distance between visitor and visited which characterizes modern tourism, and there are certain standard ways in which this distance is maintained. They create a very measured, controlled relationship between visitor and visited. And they are important for this book for two reasons; they profoundly affect the way human beings today experience the physical environment, and, even more importantly, they involve a particular dehumanizing of relationships between human beings.

Relating by photographing

Almost by definition the tourist visits places he does not know. He is not familiar with the way of life and he most likely will not have sufficient time to acquaint himself with it. The American or Japanese tourist visiting Oxford really has no more clue about its undergraduate life than the London typist visiting a Cornish fishing village understands the culture of Cornish fishermen and their wives. The situation is potentially most uncomfortable, and the most common response is to take a photograph. The critic Susan Sontag is surely right when she says in her book *On Photography*:

'Most tourists feel compelled to put the camera
between themselves and whatever is remarkable
that they encounter. Unsure of other responses,
they take a picture. This gives shape to
experience: stop, take a picture, and move on.'

The camera literally places a distance between you and the subject. It provides the appearance of participation, without the reality.

Last summer I saw a lovely little tragi-comic cameo illustrating this. I was spending a few days in the Bodleian Library at the University of Oxford, doing some preparatory work on this book. I was sitting outside the Radcliffe Camera section of the library eating my sandwiches one lunchtime, looking over the lawn that separates the Bodleian from Great St Mary's Church. It was examination time, and on the lawn were some under-graduates in examination gowns celebrating the completion of their exams in the traditional manner by drinking champagne from the bottle, and by photographing each other in this revelry. Around the corner came a guided group of foreign tourists, and they stopped at the appointed place by the lawn while the guide pointed out the architectural and historic merits of the Bodleian. The tourists were clearly interested also in the ritual activities of the students on the lawn. Too good to be missed, a sponta-neous display by the natives, it had to be photographed. So one of the tourists advanced slightly and aimed his camera. But for once the natives had cameras too! One of the students advanced toward the photographer-tourist, preparing to take a photograph of *him*. The tourist clearly saw the joke, and advanced further until the two were lens-to-lens. Laughing, they took their re-spective photographs. The tourists reassembled, while the stu-dents went off enthusiastically, saying 'let's go tourist baiting'.

The point of the story is this: neither of them had anything to say to each other. Neither of them knew how to relate to the other, except by photographing him. For the student this was an amusing interlude in his celebrations; for the tourist, it was the primary activity that he had come to England for.

Photography reduces the anxiety inherent in the tourist–native encounter because the tourist becomes preoccupied with the purely technical, and therefore emotionally undemanding, problem of getting the best photograph. This affects the tourist's relation not only to the peoples he visits, but also the places he visits. There is no awe, no fear in the presence of the Alps, the Niagara Falls, or Old Faithful, merely the technical question of the right moment to shoot, the right exposure, the right position to shoot from.

A nice example of this was displayed before me recently on a train journey from Birmingham to Bristol. It was late afternoon, and a dramatic sunset was forming over the striking silhouette of the Malvern Hills. Two tourists sitting opposite each other by the window were in the classic positions of long-distance railway travellers: one slumped asleep, the other engrossed in a novel. The novel reader noticed the forming sunset, woke the other and they both took out their cameras. They spent about five minutes adjusting their camera settings and waiting for the right moment, then took their photographs, and within seconds were back in their classic positions as though nothing had happened. The sunset went on for another twenty minutes.

At Ayers Rock, the main tourist attraction of central Australia, the visitors are actually shown the best spot to photograph the Rock from, and are told by the hotelier the exact moment during sunrise when they should shoot. Then they get into their buses and move on. While the tourist to Milford Sound in New Zealand must time his shots to the unpredictable weather, the effect is the same – a preoccupation with taking routinely ordinary photographs of Mitre Peak to the exclusion of its total setting, the stunningly beautiful Fiordland of the South Island.

The *process* of taking photographs protects the visitor from real encounter and awe, the stuff of which profound memories are made. (What is remembered from a holiday instead, as is well known, are not the photographed highlights but the things that go wrong.) Indeed, the tourist taking a photograph is often not really interacting with the place he is ostensibly photographing. Much more, he is interacting with the family or fellow tourists who usually make up the foreground of the picture, and implicitly with the folks back home to whom it will eventually be shown. The aim is to demonstrate that they have been there and that they enjoyed themselves. Often what matters is that it is a good photograph of one's party, sometimes to such an extent that the actual place need only be just recognizable; *it* need not be well photographed.

Even when the tourist is more seriously concerned with photographing the view, he does not really look at the view in its own terms. His senses do not really grapple with what there is to be experienced in it. Rather, he assesses it in terms of whether or not it will make a good photograph. If it will not, then he dismisses it, and looks no further; if it will, then he explores only those aspects that will make a photograph. It was because I realized how much I was missing that I gave up photography several years ago, and since then it is as though my eyes have been opened, not to mention my ears and other senses. I can now see beauty in things which I had previously dismissed because they would not make a good photo. (I grant that the *good* photographer sees and photographs beauty in the mundane, and can open the eyes of others to such beauty, but 99 per cent of camera owners are bad photographers.)

The *product* of the tourist's photography is a set of beautiful images to be shown to the folks back home. By selecting the pretty and omitting the ugly, photography renders the world beautiful; this is just what people in a humanistic society whose optimism is as frail as ever need to know.

Susan Sontag considers that photography also renders the world beautiful in a more subtle way. It is possible to take a bad photograph, but she thinks that it is not possible to take an ugly photograph. Photography renders ugly subjects beautiful; even 'social conscience' pictures of slums and refugees which may be shocking or disturbing nevertheless create beauty. Indeed, were there no beauty in the starving child or the dying soldier, there would be no pathos. What the photographer of the ugly is saying is, 'I find that ugly thing – beautiful'.

So, photography and tourism are eminently suited one to another, for they both make the world beautiful. Sontag senses the link in her statement that 'through the camera people become tourists of reality'. Tourists photograph, and photographers become tourists.

Reduction to the visual

The camera encourages the tourist to view reality as a visual phenomenon. Of the five senses, only sight and sound can be easily captured, taken home and stored indefinitely. You can't take a taste home like you can a picture. Taste, touch and smell are rather private sensations which may not necessarily be shared with others present, and are very difficult to communicate to others afterwards.

There is a kind of pragmatism here which is posing as an absolute. The visual is the aspect of a place which we happen to be able to record and capture most easily, but we are not content to enjoy it for what it is – one aspect among several. No, the tourist has to fool himself that this aspect is the essence of the place, that he has captured the heart of the thing. To admit otherwise would be to put in jeopardy the whole enterprise of tourism as a grasping of the world.

The photographer-tourist willingly confuses appearance for reality. Susan Sontag again:

'Photography implies that we know about the
world if we accept it as the camera records it. But
this is the opposite of understanding, which starts
from *not* accepting the world as it looks. All
possibility of understanding is rooted in the ability
to say no. Strictly speaking, one never understands
anything from a photograph.'

This is how photography makes the world beautiful: by making appearance look like reality.

Not that photography invented this trick. Our old friends the eighteenth-century landscape gardeners have a lot to answer for. Before the early eighteenth century the finest humanly-created landscapes in Europe involved some combination of the natural with the human, of the purely visual with a pleasure in fields well tilled. 'The English eighteenth century was unique in giving more weight to the visual composition than to husbandry. Trees pleasantly grouped in grassland became the essential features of the country park, while grazing became subsidiary.'[1] Despite drastic changes in fashion in the course of the century from the formal to the informal to the picturesque, the debate about landscape in England continued in purely visual terms. Jane Austen lampoons this in *Northanger Abbey* (1818):

'A lecture on the picturesque immediately
followed, in which his instructions were so clear
that she soon began to see beauty in everything
admired by him, and her attention was so earnest
that he became perfectly satisfied of her having a
great deal of natural taste. He talked of
foregrounds, distances, and second distances –
side-screens and perspectives . . .'

With this reduction of landscape to the purely visual, the English were well fitted to become the first mass tourists.

Of the five senses, the visual is the one which requires least involvement with the subject. Taste and touch, for example, involve physical contact, and this is not necessarily desired by the tourist. Every tourist given the chance will take a picture of a slum child in Calcutta or of a lion in a safari park, but few would wish to touch either. You can *see* perfectly well while remaining in your vehicle. It is this that makes safaris and safari parks so popular and, for the visitor, such an 'authentic' experience. They depend on the belief that reality may be reduced to the visual because the visual is its essence. Without this belief, safaris would be most dissatisfying, for the visitor does not touch, taste or smell the animals and may well not even hear them above the noise of the vehicle engine and through the tightly shut windows. Yet this is deemed a more 'real' experience than the zoo in which you can smell and hear the animals, and in which there is at least a possibility of one of them biting your finger off.

So when reality is reduced to the visual the tourist has the protection of distance that he requires, and the assurance that he is experiencing the real thing. It tells him that he need not touch in order to have an authentic experience.

This emphasis on what the tourist is looking at takes his attention away from the means by which he is able to look at it. He sees the view or the historic monument, but he is blind to all the surrounding paraphernalia which has enabled him to get there and see it: the parked cars, the clicking cameras, the restaurant, the plastic macs, and so on. His is not a multi-dimensional experience of the whole scene, but a reduction of it to one visual object. (This explains why postcards and calendar pictures of tourist attractions also omit, if at all possible, what a visitor from Mars would see as the most prominent features – the cars, the hotels, and the tourists themselves. The postcard does not depict the attraction as it is, but as it appears to the tourist.)

This relationship to a physical scene may be contrasted with that enjoyed in several activities which may not be accurately described as tourism. Many hill-walkers enjoy a multi-sense experience; they relish the sensuous feel of the rocky path or soggy bog through the soles of their boots, they taste the clear mountain air as they breath it deep into their lungs, and they may even enjoy the feel of the rain and the mist. Sunbathers relish the penetration of the sun's rays on the flesh, a tactile experience which involves a direct contact with nature. This is comparable with the rock-climber's delicate and sensuous contact with the rock. Motor-cycling, ski-ing and a host of other sports involve this multi-sense relationship with the environment.

Children are natural multi-sense explorers of their physical environment. The child's contact with the natural world is well depicted in the illustrations to some children's books, especially fairy stories. In *The Water Fairies* by Molly Brett, the 'fairies' (who are actually children) are shown dancing with frogs, lying fishing on a water lily leaf, sitting asleep within a water lily flower, riding on the back of a flying kingfisher or hanging onto its tail, using a half walnut shell as a coracle, and being pulled through the air by a dragonfly. Pictures such as this are very sensuous: touch and intimate contact are as important as sight in the child's experience of his environment. But we adults dissuade the child who wants to pull a worm apart, and I suspect our dissuasion has as much to do with our repression of this tactile exploration of nature as with any concern for the worm. In vain, parents try to get their young children to appreciate landscape and views.

Children can reveal to us how limited is our largely visual perception of the environment. I recall visiting a major exhibition of Barbara Hepworth sculptures in the Botanic Gardens in Edinburgh. I looked at them from this way and that, but could make little sense of them. So, having time on my hands; I sat down and decided to watch the other visitors and see if I could learn from them how to relate to these curious objects. The result was fascinating. Almost without exception, the adults were as puzzled as I. At each sculpture, they peered, frowned and moved quickly on to the next. Almost without exception, the children knew what to do: they climbed on them, crawled through the holes in them, felt the texture of the surface, and were utterly fascinated by them. It seemed the adults were unshakable in the opinion that works of art are *visual* objects. The children clearly had not yet learnt this, and so were not prevented from enjoying the sculptures. Having learnt the lesson, I then wandered round, treating the sculptures as primarily tactile objects. Not that I crawled through any holes, but I relished the feel of the bronze, I got down on my hands and knees to view one sculpture through the holes in another; I even smelt them. I was immensely grateful to the children.

One of the few memories I have of my young childhood is of visiting Stonehenge. It was a misty morning as we walked across the moor, and then these vast stones came looming out of the mist. I recall touching them and feeling the mystery; looking up from the base of each stone and *feeling* its immensity; putting my nose to them and *smelling* their age. You can no longer do this. Because of vandalism and the pressure of millions of feet on the turf, they have been ringed by a rope fence and you can only view from forty yards. Whatever the reason, the effect is the same: a truly remarkable phenomenon has been reduced to its visual aspect, to something which can be photographed, visually wrapped up and taken home. One more wonder of the world to add to the collection of photographs at home. One more sight to be ticked off the list. Not in vain do we talk of seeing the *sights*, and *sightseeing*.

Tourists are sightseers. Rockclimbers, sunbathers and hill-walkers are not. And children make bad sightseers, as many an irritated vacationing parent knows only too well.

In chapter four, I described how the sacred places which so often become tourist attractions are conceived of as works of art. The 'picture postcard' English village is reduced from a living, economic, political and social entity to a purely aesthetic object. I mentioned two features of works of art as conceived today: they require an attitude of disinterestedness in order to be appreciated, and they can only be seen as art by ignoring the context in which they were produced. It should be clear now how these features of art are eminently suited for tourism, for both art and tourism involve a certain distance from reality. The reduction of the tourist site to a work of art removes it from the ongoing life of the local community, which is essential if the visitor is to assimilate it in the few minutes available to him. It also removes it from the real-life concerns of the visitor, who is not materially affected one way or the other by the existence of the sight.

Our discussion so far is well summarized in the modern tourist's relationship to the medieval cathedral. The building undergoes a triple reduction: to an aesthetic object, to a visual object, and to an object which can be captured in a photograph. For the medieval visitor, though, the cathedral was a complex set of symbols informing him of spiritual truths:

'The vertical cosmos of medieval man is
dramatically symbolized by pointed arches, towers,
and spires that soar. The Gothic cathedral baffles
the modern man. A tourist with his camera may
be impressed by the beauty of the nave with its
aisles, transepts, radiating chapels, and the span of
the vaults. Should he seek a position to set up his
camera, he will find that there is no privileged

position from which all these features may be
seen. To see a Gothic interior properly one has to
move about and turn one's head. Outside the
cathedral the modern tourist may be able to get a
good picture of the total structure from a distance.
But in medieval times this was seldom possible.
Other buildings cluttered around the edifice and
blocked the distant view. Moreover, to see the
cathedral from a distance would diminish its
impact of bulk and verticality. The details of its
facade would no longer be visible. The medieval
cathedral was meant to be experienced; it was a
dense text to be read with devout attention and
not an architectural form to be merely seen. In
fact some figures and decorations could not be
seen at all. They were made for the eyes of God.'[2]

This quote shows how the tourist's accumulation of knowledge
and experiences is fundamentally false. If he so misunderstands
something from his own western tradition and from his own
religion, how much more will he be fooling himself if he thinks
he has understood anything of non-western peoples? But so long
as he *thinks* he understands, and nobody disabuses him, then all
will be well.

Staged authenticity

The tourist's experience feels authentic, but in fact it is not.
This is quite obvious not only to the natives, but also to other
visitors who do not relate to the place in the role of tourist (and
my discussion of mountaineers and children has suggested that
tourism is *not* the only way visitors can relate to the places they
visit). These other visitors tend to look down on 'mere tourists'
for the superficiality of their relationship to the place. The person who spends a vacation grape-picking in a French vineyard
feels one up on the tourists who come for half an hour to take
photographs and then move on. Likewise mountaineers despise
tourists who ascend the mountain by cable car, gawp from the
mountain-top hotel, take their pictures (of each other *in* the

mountains rather than of the mountains themselves) and descend the way they came up:

'The Diavolezza hotel was nearly full. Most of the
people were holidaymakers in organized groups on
sightseeing excursions. That way they could come
to no harm and they would miss nothing. There
was no need to make elaborate plans in advance,
or have to think for themselves once they reached
their destination, as we were bound to. Engaging
them in conversation one soon grasped their point
of view, which was intelligent in the light of their
aspirations and conception of a holiday and often
entertaining when they related experiences.
Almost without exception they could not visualize
themselves acting on their own initiative, at least
when the object was seeing mountains at close
quarters; and although many of them would have
dearly loved to have trodden the higher places
their eyes were constantly directed to, they were
quite incapable of summoning the imagination and
powers of leadership required to bridge the gap
between their level and ours . . . A few plucky
ones would follow guides to the summit of Palü;
many more would file down to the Boval hut
across the glacier; as many again would rise early
to witness the rose of sunrise dapple the shining
cirque of peaks, take a late breakfast and return
to the valley on the cableway situated a few yards
from the door.'[3]

The contrast being made here is with the mountaineer's knowledge of the mountains, which has to be tested against reality every moment he is on a climb. If his knowledge is not authentic, then he is dead. He feels at home in the high hills, and feels he is a part of them. The tourist's involvement with the hills is superficial: if not assisted by the cable car he would collapse from exhaustion, if not shepherded by the guide he would surely lose himself or fall down a crevasse. The mountaineer pities the tourist for the superficiality of his relationship with the very place where he is seeking some respite from the superficiality of everyday life. Above all he mocks the tourist industry for putting the whole show on; in American sociologist Dean Maccannell's phrase, for providing 'staged authenticity'. Tourists, for their part, are willing dupes.

This should not surprise us. Tourism provides the picture of the world that the tourist wants to see. This is not so different from the way in which newspapers and television portray the world not as it really is, but as their mass audiences want to see it.[4] The techniques are different, but the effect is the same: to enable the recipient to feel he has some grasp of the world, a grasp which somehow justifies his own values and way of life. The successful tour is completed by the sentiment 'It's good to be home' or 'There's no place like home'. The glacier tour may give you a mild thrill, the television news may show starving children in Cambodia, but at the end of the day you are glad you can curl up in your own bed in Surbiton, London or Scarsdale, New York.

The golden rule for the tourist guide is: never upset or disturb them, for they are on vacation and want to enjoy it. Always confirm them in their own values and their image of themselves.

Following the photographic incident at the Bodleian Library, I decided to join a guided tour of the Oxford colleges in order to discover the portrait of college life given to tourists. The guide's technique, it seemed, was to relate whatever was being looked at to the tourists' own experience. Steeped as the colleges are in history, the trick was to start the story of each college with some incident involving a famous person the tourists were bound to have heard of. 'Henry VIII stayed here. I find that overseas visitors have always heard of him'.

History for most people consists of a few dots – for the English, 1066, the signing of Magna Carta, King Henry VIII and his six wives, the battles of Trafalgar and Waterloo – with vast empty spaces in between. Certainly there is no sense of the forces that relate the dots and drive history along. The guided tour took some of the dots and began to flesh them out a little, by relating an incident involving King Henry or the Duke of Wellington, or famous literary figures such as Shelley or Lewis Carroll. It provided no radically new information, and certainly did nothing to challenge the tourists' conception of English history: all it did was to confirm that the dots were the right dots and were what make sense of college life in Oxford. For the tourist, the college buildings provided material evidence that his view of history was correct.

Perhaps not much more could have been done in the short space of two hours, and certainly any good teacher starts with what knowledge the pupil already has and builds on it. But the question is, *what* does he build on it? Does he move on to provide new information which enables the pupil to view critically his original starting point? The tourist guide does not, and evidence for this is found in the golden rule for the guided. You may ask the guide to amplify, you may even add some information of your own. ('The spire looks very much like the one at Salisbury we saw yesterday.' To which the guide may reply, 'That's right, they were both built by the same master mason.') But *the one thing you may not do is to contradict the guide*. Intellectual visitors may comment among themselves that they think the guide has got it wrong or talk to the guide privately during the tour, but they never challenge the guide publicly in the presence of the group, for that would raise the disturbing possibility that history may not be as it seems to be.

The fact that the ultimate function of tourism is to confirm, rather than to provide escape from, the person's view of life, is indicated by much of the tourists' behaviour. Not only are they glad when they get home, but often their major activities after photography are writing postcards and purchasing souvenirs and gifts for the folks back home. Through the postcard they maintain contact with their home base, and among some tourists this desire to remain in touch seems almost compulsive. At the same time, the postcard's idealized image of the place being visited provides just the image that is required. And the postcard which drops through the letterbox in no way hints that this idealization has been staged. Even if the tourist himself can see through it, on return home he is surrounded by the many friends, relatives and workmates who have received the postcards. They inform him of what authentically beautiful and interesting places he has been to; or at very least they have been primed by the postcard picture into becoming a gullible audience who cannot see through the show.

The major activity, photography, also helps to keep the tourist in touch with himself. Taking a photograph is the sort of technical operation that we engage in every day: programming the washing machine, putting a record on the turntable, operating the lathe in the factory. It is a familiar mode of operation, and through it the tourist reminds himself that he is still himself. Taking photographs not only puts a protective distance between you and the dancing natives or the Niagara Falls, it also reminds you that ultimate reality is the industrial, technological society of which you are a member. The natives and the falls are but an appearance or at most an abnormal curiosity; *your* way of life (whether as male lathe operator or housewifely washing machine operator) is normal reality. Sontag again, on the tourist's compulsion to take photographs:

'The method especially appeals to people
handicapped by a ruthless work ethic – Germans,
Japanese, and Americans. Using a camera
appeases the anxiety which the work-driven feel
about not working when they are on vacation and
supposed to be having fun. They have something
to do that is like a friendly imitation of work: they
can take pictures.'

The leisured life of the native may challenge the anthropology student's commitment to the western notion of work, and the marvellous interrelationship of nature may cause the ecologist to question the superiority of technology, but neither challenge the tourist. His camera asserts the primacy of work and of technology: it provides the lens through which he views what had the potential of challenging him, and thereby the challenge is never seen.

Moral detachment

This inability really to grasp the place and the culture is further fostered by one other feature of tourism. The tourist's relation to the sights is a-moral. Donning the role of tourist involves putting on spectacles which cut out any moral vision. A modern Christian tourist visiting the Colosseum and other pagan buildings in Rome feels little of what these places of persecution meant for the early Christians. One wonders even about the feelings of today's visitors to Auschwitz where 'the underlying horror of the place seems diminished by the souvenir stands, Pepsi-Cola signs and the tourist attraction atmosphere'.[5] If a tourist *did* feel morally outraged enough actually to *do* something, then in that moment he would cease to be a tourist. Or if he passionately *approved* of the life displayed before him, then in that moment he would have 'gone native' and most likely he would soon be putting his home up for sale and moving to join the natives, or at least giving up touring the world and returning year after year to the place he had fallen in love with.

This moral detachment is shared by those photographers who are not official tourists, a fact which provides yet more evidence of the essential similarity of tourism and photography. I recall watching live on television with some emotion the funeral of President Tito of Yugoslavia. Here were a million or more people, visibly moved to the depths of their national and individual being: ordinary peasants weeping, officials and soldiers marching solemnly. All, that is, except the journalists with their cameras: holding them high above their heads to get a picture over the crowd, wandering around at will (unlike anybody else) photographing visiting heads of state, even sometimes lounging with hands in pockets when they had nothing to photograph. They were essentially tourists. Perhaps the same is true of war photographers.

And yet there is a paradox, for, although the *process* of taking photographs is without morality, the *product* – the pictures themselves – can be intensely moving and moral. Indeed, it was only through the television pictures that I myself could participate in the emotion of the funeral. Perhaps this is what distinguishes the war photographer's or journalist's pictures from the tourist's: the professional's pictures have the potential to move, to contain a moral message and to challenge. The tourist's do not.

It has been said that the tourist is the modern day pilgrim. Certainly there is a lot of the pilgrim in the tourist, and a lot of the tourist in the pilgrim. And when one considers the provision by tour operators in Arab countries of pilgrimages to Mecca, one sees that the two roles can overlap. But the moral detachment of the tourist does not characterize the pilgrim, and the social detachment of the pilgrim – the way he has separated himself from his own society – does not characterize the tourist. Victor and Edith Turner in their study of Christian pilgrimages have shown that in medieval times the pilgrimage was quite an anomaly in society. Most pilgrimages were not officially sanctioned by the church, and pilgrim sites grew (and still do) in a remarkably uncontrolled way. The pilgrimage was individually willed by the pilgrim, and was not an essential requirement of official religion. While on the journey, the pilgrim was remarkably free of social ties; indeed, for the average feudal serf, it would be the only time of his life that he would be free of social obligation – an experience of explosive potential for someone living in an otherwise very controlled society.

The contrast with pilgrimages highlights the essential nature of tourism. In pilgrimage the person finds the centre of his life out there, away from his home society; this challenges the claim of his own society to be ultimate reality. The tourist does not find the centre of life out there on his travels. He simply looks through his own cultural spectacles and returns home, confirmed in his knowledge that home is the centre of the world. Tourism enables him to feel at home in the big, wide world.

Of course, there are exceptions: the tourist visiting India who makes his home there in order to learn yoga and the sitar; the visitor to Israel who returns year after year to spend time on a kibbutz. But these people have ceased to be tourists. There are also those I would call travellers rather than tourists; those who travel specifically in order to have their eyes opened. In the late 1960s it became reasonably common for young people to travel in order to 'find themselves'; this was not tourism aimed at reaffirming their worldview, for they were still forming their worldview. They displayed a genuine openness to and willingness to learn from the societies they visited. Few went native and failed to return; many came back able to see their own society afresh and to see their own role in that society more clearly. The contrast between the tourist who looks without seeing and the traveller who spends time in order to see and to understand is well put by a Nepalese sherpa commenting on the escalating numbers of visitors to the high Himalaya:

'Many people come looking, looking, taking
pictures. Too many people, no good . . . Some
people come see. Good!'[6]

Chapter Ten
SYMBOLS OF FREEDOM

'A healthy being welcomes constraint and
freedom, the boundedness of place and the
exposure of space.'

Yi-Fu Tuan, Space and Place

Place has to do with rootedness, with home. Because they are
specific and material, places are reassuring, for they give solidity
to existence. They make culture and its categories visible and
stable.

This is all deeply reassuring, but what about the desire to
transcend everyday life? What of criticism of one's culture?
What of the desire to break free? How can such feelings be
expressed in terms of the environment? This is where *spaces*
come in, for a space has no categories. It has not yet had human
meanings imposed on it in such a firm and rigid way that it has
become a definable place. Place is space plus added human
meaning. Undefined space is therefore both a symbol of freedom
and transcendence, and a threat. Space retains an openness,
waiting for humans to do with it what they will.[1]

Nomadic societies, whose members are constantly on the
move experience space daily. They put immense symbolic value
on the security of particular places, such as the oasis. In their
religions, god is associated with a particular place: the tree or
rock of the African tribe, the high place of the Canaanites.

Settled societies, however, possess static places in abundance.
What takes on special symbolic value for them is open space.
Once the children of Israel had settled down in the land, the

wilderness was where the radical prophets often went to pray and find inspiration. In the medieval market town choc-a-bloc with home-places, the one vast soaring architectural *space* was the cathedral. In many religions the sky is a symbol for God. By the same measure, space can also symbolize danger for settled societies; undefined and uncontrolled, it is an offence to an ordered, stable world.

Although not always expressed in terms immediately recognizable as religious, today space still provides a powerful symbol of freedom (and of threat). If one is to feel truly at home in the universe, one needs not only physical security and order, but also bolt holes, places of escape where there is the possibility of transcending the daily order. The Robin Hood story provides one such symbol of freedom: in an agricultural society in which law and order were embodied in well-tilled fields, it was the forest which provided a niche for rebels and freedom lovers. This symbolism of the woods has been carried on through literature to this day, along with the complementary mythology of the forest as the home of uncontrolled forces and as a threat (for example, the fairy story of Little Red Riding Hood). The woods meant freedom for Robin, but menace for the Sheriff of Nottingham.

In this chapter, I will look at how freedom and danger are symbolized by three particular sorts of environment: the city, the street, and moving on.[2]

The city

As with the domestic house, the function of the earliest cities was as much symbolic as physical, but the symbolism is very different from that of the house. From earliest times the city was, in Lewis Mumford's words, a magnet rather than a container. It was not so much a place where people lived as where they met, traded, worshipped, and buried their dead. In the Bible, for example, Jerusalem is almost always described in such terms and one is hard put to think of biblical characters (apart from kings and courtiers) who actually lived there.

Cities have always attracted people on the move, dissidents and outcasts. In the city they find the freedom to innovate, to practise their religion or to seek employment, while such opportunities may not be available within the much more ordered village or small town. In the medieval city, merchants found freedom from feudal restrictions; in the American city, businessmen seeking fame and fortune find opportunity; poor immigrants make the big city their first port of call. The city is on the move, and so are its inhabitants – geographically, socially, politically or religiously.

The city destabilizes traditional ways of life. All societies have contact through trade or war with other societies, but this kind of contact produces only a superficial acquaintance with them. Short of being conquered by another race, it is only in the city that you actually start living with other cultures, and only then do you have to take them seriously. This creates friction and disorder and vitality. There are more social niches available in the urban cultural muddle, which is why freedom-seekers flock to the city. At its extreme there is complete anonymity; the soul-lessness of the city reduces it from·a place to a meaningless space, in which the lack of observation by others provides freedom from being bugged by others.

This cultural variety is also why the city is not a place many people raise a family if they have any choice in the matter. Bringing up children involves teaching them the ways of one's own culture, and this is not made easy by the presence of other races and cultures. Parents want order, stability and security for their family; these features are embodied in the house, but not in the city. The city may be an exciting place to visit, but the suburbs provide the ordered, controllable environment which families desire, where all their neighbours are culturally and racially just like themselves.

This attitude avoids the moral challenge of the city. Jesus' parable of the Good Samaritan is the product of an urban society, it is set on a road between the two cities of Jerusalem and Jericho. The variety of classes, castes and races who pass along the road would only be found together in an urban society. You would never find such a variety in a suburban side street – at least not if the residents had their way. The parable teaches that love may come from the most unexpected source, even from the very class one cannot abide. Jesus' interrogator, who prompted the parable by asking 'Who is my neighbour?', was trying (like the suburban family) to control and limit the class of people he wanted as neighbours and to whom he would have to be neighbour. Jesus' point is that human love can only really be tested and displayed when this selectivity is absent. Suburbia stifles the moral potential of human beings; the city opens the possibility both of practical love (embodied in the Samaritan) and of the depths of dehumanization (embodied in the other travellers who ignored the wounded man).

In a remarkable book, *The Uses of Disorder*, the sociologist Richard Sennett has translated this truth into secular terms. (Incidentally, he seems unaware his ideas find their ancestry in Jesus' teaching.) He examines city life and the development of the character of the individual. In the culturally mixed inner city, people have to face up to the fact that not everyone has the same values and lifestyle as themselves. They have to cope with the West Indian party at 3 a.m. in the apartment upstairs, with the homosexual couple in the flat downstairs, and the youngster next door who loves revving his motorbike at all hours. There is no escape, and Sennett believes that it would be a good thing to limit the role of the police so that neighbours had to sort out neighbourly conflicts themselves.

In the suburbs though, social uniformity is the norm, so residents gain little experience of how to relate to those with different lifestyles, different cultures and different values. Consequently, they come to fear those who are different; they do not know how to handle them, and so they come to see them as a threat. It is in socially uniform middle class suburbs and solidly working class areas that there lie the seeds of prejudice against despised groups, and from these areas come calls for authoritarian imposition of law and order. Although most people believe that racial tension is generated in the mixed-up inner city areas, the exact opposite may well be the case: it is in the solidly white areas that prejudice and fear are *generated*, though they may be *expressed* in the mixed areas.

The city represents one of the fundamental problems of a mobile, expanding world: how do we relate to those we disagree with? Living next door to such people can provide challenge, vitality, life and the opportunity for both moral growth and real grass roots democracy. The question is, do we want such things? Do we want such people?

The street

If the city provides vitality and excitement over against the security and order of the home, then it is the street that epitomizes this vitality for many young people. The street is where the action is for many youngsters who are bored with the order of home, and want to shed its security. What they look for in the street is well expressed in British sociologist Paul Corrigan's article *Doing Nothing*:

'In fighting boredom the kids do not choose the
street as a wonderfully lively place, rather they
look on it as the place where there is the most
chance that something will happen. Doing nothing
on the street must be compared with the
alternatives: for example, knowing that nothing
will happen with Mum and Dad in the front room;
being almost certain that the youth club will be
full of boredom. This makes the street the place
where something might just happen, if not this
Saturday, then surely next.'[3]

The street provides just the possibility that something might happen. There is diversity there, and the possibility of the unexpected, of something weird happening, something that is remarkable – worth remarking on and talking about.

Peter Marsh's[4] study of violence among English football fans, came to a conclusion that complements Corrigan's. It is not that football stands and terraces are utterly disorderly places where bizarre things go on all the time. Rather the reverse; there is a coherent social order on the terraces. The young fans know this, and they know that few people get hurt even when things get out of hand. But the fans, like Corrigan's kids, are looking for excitement. The media provide a ready rhetoric about the terraces being violent unpredictable places, and, thus encouraged, the fans are more than ready to believe this is true. The terraces, like Corrigan's streets on a Saturday night, *symbolize* disorder for the kids, even though they are not disorderly.

This points to the important conclusion that, whether or not places like streets and football terraces actually *are* disorderly, some people (the media and some youngsters) *want to believe* they are, and some of these (the youngsters) want to participate in that disorder, whether it exists or not. Such places are powerful symbols.

Of course, there is a sense in which Corrigan's and Marsh's adolescents are doing what all children do: going out to play. For children, 'indoors' represents security and shelter and being under the protection and authority of adults. 'Going out to play' for the child (shortened to 'going out' for the adolescent) involves a greater or lesser adventure in the big world, a world whose order has not yet been fully grasped by the child and which therefore offers the excitement of disorder.

The street has taken on a particular meaning in many working class areas of post-war Britain.[5] In the older working class areas of British cities, in which families had lived in the same streets for generations, the life of the local community was lived to a large extent on the doorstep, in the corner shop and on the street (nostalgically portrayed today in the television series *Coronation Street*). The old terraced houses, often slums, were no place for socializing in. Neighbours often supported each other in the day-to-day problems of life, financial and emotional.

In the 1950s and 60s, however, the widespread desire for a better standard of accommodation led to the destruction of such communities as old neighbourhoods were demolished and new tower blocks and estates built in their place. This coincided with some increase in affluence, which led many working class families to adopt a more private family life, relying on the nuclear family for meaning, support and companionship, in preference to the extended family or the neighbourhood. The family life of husband, wife and dependent children became emotionally more intense: tensions generated by the family had to be solved or relieved within the family. On the good side, many couples wanted this kind of relationship, enjoyed consuming their new found affluence together, and certainly were glad that mother-in-law was at arm's length and that they could sort out their own problems themselves. On the bad side, it could lead to impasses in the emotional life of the family. With no outside relief, the only solution is for some members to storm out of the home – in the form of a spouse leaving for good, a member of the family going mad, or an offspring spending all his spare time on the street.

At the same time that the youngster was maybe finding the home emotionally too intense, he found to his relief that the street had been emptied of all the adults and old busybodies who had occupied it in pre-war days. Here he was free from adult supervision, and could think of the street as his very own domain. Here was freedom. (As a consequence, this is also where the youngster is most likely to commit offences. The most common location for serious *adult* offences, by contrast, is the home. In the home the adult is most free from observation and restraint by others, and in the home the sometimes unbearable emotional closeness of modern private family life can generate wife beating and child beating.)

So the street has become the main location for *cultural resistance*, protests by young people against the dominant culture of their country. It is on the streets that kids on motor cycles not only declare their masculinity (which is actually a very conventional thing to do) but declare it in a way they know will annoy adults who value a bit of peace and quiet. It is on the street that punks know they will shock grown-ups by their dress and behaviour. It was in the streets and on the beaches that Mods and Rockers engaged in their ritual battles in the 1960s.

In the street riots which erupted in several British cities in the summer of 1981 this cultural resistance linked up with the *political* resistance that urban streets have witnessed repeatedly since the days of ancient Rome. The urban street is the classic location for the political demonstration, for the assertion by the populace of its freedom to voice its objection to the policies of its leaders. Eighteenth-century London, nineteenth-century Paris and twentieth-century Prague all demonstrate the near universal potential of the street as a symbol of freedom and resistance, reflected in the phrase 'to take to the streets'. Napoleon tried to deny this role to the street by rebuilding Paris with boulevardes long and broad and straight enough for cavalry and gunners to be able to control the crowds, but he could not succeed entirely in this. The symbolic meaning of the urban street seems to endure.

Moving on

Those who find life and freedom in the city or the street do have homes to go back to. They are still rooted in a place, and this they may find irksome. Their freedom is not total. The most radical solution is to abandon home altogether, to take to the road. If the urban street marks a temporary freedom for the rebellious adolescent, the open road represents a life of freedom for the dissident adult. The nomad in an otherwise settled society is rather difficult for the forces of conformity to control; you cannot pin down someone who is always on the move. Moreover, if someone is able to carry on moving, this symbolizes the fact that he has not yet conformed to a society which demands conformity.

This is well understood by many working class 'non-academic' pupils in British secondary schools who are on the move throughout the school day:

'Some of the lads develop the ability of moving
about the school at their own will to a remarkable
degree. They construct virtually their own day
from what is offered by the school. Truancy is
only one relatively unimportant and crude variant
of this principle of self-direction which ranges
across vast chunks of the syllabus and covers many
diverse activities: being free out of class, being in
class and doing no work, being in the wrong class,
roaming the corridors looking for excitement,
being asleep in private. The core skill which
articulates these possibilities is being able to get

out of any given class: the preservation of personal
mobility.'[6]

The author goes on to describe how this assertion of freedom
through mobility lasts only a few years in the youngster's life,
for it induces in him a naive confidence that he can beat the
system, a confidence which causes him to accept eagerly the
dead-end jobs on the factory floor that the job market allocates
to him. A year or two later he realizes he is trapped.

Gypsies make a more sustained attempt to assert their freedom to pursue an alternative way of life. They have behind
them a history and a long cultural tradition which the subculture
of working class schoolchildren lacks. Some travelling people,
especially the women, desire a house and a settled life so that
their children can receive the benefits of the state education
system, but others doubt the possibility of continuing their
unique way of life once they have moved into a permanent
house. There is surely much wisdom in their doubts. Why else
would the authorities want to provide fixed caravan sites and
houses? Surely in order to control more easily what to a
bureaucratic, rooted society is a thorn in the flesh.

Antagonism to gypsies is typically expressed in terms of physical pollution: they are 'dirty', they leave 'litter' about, they are
a 'health hazard', and so forth. But as we have seen before,
accusations of physical pollution are expressions of more deep-
rooted conflicts, fears and contradictions. The challenge of the
gypsies is that they demonstrate the possibility of alternative
values, and more important still they demonstrate a freedom
which people envy, and therefore resent.

Whereas the open road symbolizes freedom to the modern
nomad, the nomad symbolizes a threat for the settled. Whereas
for the nomad 'rootedness' is a property of vegetables – and
who wants to be a vegetable – for the rooted the word 'rootless'
is equally negative. The gypsies are especially challenging because, in social and family terms, they are far from rootless;
they have stronger family ties and a stronger sense of ancestry
that most non-gypsy house dwellers. The possibility of being
socially rooted without needing to be physically rooted calls into

question the whole business of living in houses, for are not houses meant to be vital for civilized family life?

In the USA, however, the modern nomad seems, in myth at any rate, curiously attractive to the settled. It is important for the identity of most white American families that they trace their family history back through various migrations within the States back to the original ancestor who crossed the ocean to come to America. These migrants are the founding fathers and mothers of the family, its heroes and heroines. Yet the reality for most Americans today is that they are relatively static. They change residence on average every four to five years, but this is usually not to a new beginning like their forefathers but from being trapped in one part of the suburban sprawl to another. Consequently there is some envy of those for whom the freedom of the road is still reality. The hobo, the gentleman of the road, has gained a certain mythical status in American culture, for he is acting out the old American myth that moving is the avenue to freedom. And no matter if the hobo does not have the most desirable character: were not the earliest settlers to America the despised dissidents of seventeenth-century Europe?

Actual hoboes and migrant workers are usually given as rough a treatment as vagrants in any society. What makes America different though is the importance of the *mythical* hobo, the man with no home. This is the hero of many a western film, classically played by Clint Eastwood or Lee Van Cleef, the man who comes from nowhere, whose home is the saddle. He sorts out the conflicts and injustices induced by property and settled-ness – cattle, gold, women, political injustice – and then rides off into the sunset. He has no commitments, no vested interests, and cannot be corrupted. So the vagrant becomes the saviour. Were he to be shown in a home of his own, he would become mortal, subject to the corruptions of ordinary men. In American culture, place represents the possibility of corruption; space represents purity.

In the Hollywood hero stakes not far behind the stranger riding into the sunset comes the cowboy. Though he is subject to the constraints of having to earn his living, he owns nothing but his horse and his gun. He is filmed under the vast open skies of the desert, usually in the saddle and rarely at home. In effect the saddle is his home, and his essential character is defined by mobility. The modern equivalent is the long-distance truck driver, and the imagery of this modern hero is identical to that of the cowboy.

American films, even if they do not feature cowboys or truck drivers, typically contain much more footage of travelling than do most English or European films. The 1950s Agatha Christie movie thriller may be located almost entirely in some decayed country mansion; artistic English films of the 1970s such as *The Go-Between* and *The Virgin and the Gypsy* are shot largely in one place. French films often remain within the confines of a single provincial town. But not so the American movie.

In particular, Hollywood has produced a type of movie uniquely its own – the movie whose story is a journey, not necessarily *to* anywhere. *Easy Rider*, *Midnight Cowboy*, *Alice Doesn't Live Here Anymore*, *Zabriski Point* have no equivalents in Europe. It is in the journey rather than the destination that the characters of such films discover what life is all about. They may well experience the persecution that actual vagrants typically *do* experience, as in *Easy Rider*, but the travellers are the heroes. They have had the guts to break away from small town America or from the big bad city and are trying to find the real America. They may be powerfully disappointed, but the message is in a long American tradition: that space is more meaningful than place, that movement reveals truth, not settledness.

It is this desire for a physical realization of personal freedom that has made the *automobile* such a cherished possession in American culture. It is one reason, too, why restrictions on its use (for example, through heavy taxation on gasoline) are politically unacceptable. The fact that many Americans love to *possess* a car but are happy merely to *rent* a house or apartment suggests that they are more concerned with freedom than with security. Like the cowboy, their true home is the driving seat, they are never more at home than when they are on the move.

In the Hollywood movie, the *back* seat of the automobile is also important, for it challenges the bed as the proper location for making love. In most human societies the sexual act, with all its implications of fertility, the future and the past, the continuity of life, stability and security, is associated with a Nature goddess of order and rootedness. Only in America, perhaps, could the sexual act be mythologically located within the automobile, symbol of transience, movement and space. From my first, and so far only, visit to the United States, the scene that I treasure most captured precisely this sense of movement and transience. One warm spring evening, we drove out of town a mile or two to attend to my host's three horses. A beautiful sunset was forming over the Kansas wheatlands. I remember the breeze rustling the few trees; the horses pawing the ground, as though a storm were coming; the wind pump whirring around; a truck driving across the horizon against the sunset. All sights and sounds of movement, of change. The only man-made things were telegraph poles along the road, and a pair of those giant grain elevators (silos) that characterize the Mid-West, like some American Stonehenge against the sky; hardly human, certainly not a home. The whole scene somehow beautiful in its loneliness.

Of course, there may be technical reasons for the movie conventions. British film makers may not have the financial resources to go roaming a continent for location shots; most Americans need an automobile to get to work, shops and friends; and teenagers who cannot use their parents' house for love-making find their car the most available alternative. But the symbolism still exists, and is consistent with the preoccupation with space in American culture generally and with place in English culture.

Freedom and order, space and place

So far the themes of space and place have been presented as in conflict, as indeed they are, for modern society has not yet resolved the tension between order and freedom. There is a constant struggle to balance the two, and this is represented in the ambiguous symbolism of many objects and places. The city, portrayed so far in this chapter as a symbol of life and diversity, also has a long tradition – certainly in the eyes of its rulers – as a manifestation of power, order and stability. Lewis Mumford in his book *The City in History* has argued that totalitarian regimes consistently build cities to secure their position over their subjects. What Mumford terms the 'Baroque' cities built in Europe from the fifteenth to the nineteenth century, epitomized perhaps by Napoleon's Paris, were designed to repress democratic freedoms and to maintain public order. The physical remains of a city – the Parthenon or the Arc de Triomphe – represent totalitarian and bureaucratic order. (The grand public buildings of the Athens of the fourth century BC involved a pride which signalled the end of that city's high period of democracy.) Cities which have contained the seeds of democracy and freedom have not had particularly grand or durable fabrics: Athenian houses of the fifth century BC Athens were little more than village huts (even though Greek philosophy and politics were at their most vibrant), the congested fire-prone apartments of the medieval trader, the modern urban ghetto and its potential for neighbourliness.

Good town planners have been concerned with just this problem of order versus life. They know that unplanned cities are alive but chaotic, while planned cities can be orderly but dead. How can order be maintained at the same time as diversity? How can they deal rationally with complexity? How can they allow growth while retaining coherence? These were the issues that concerned Ebenezer Howard, the inventor of the garden city. His real goal was not, as is commonly believed, to inject a little greenery into the urban scene, but to retain a vibrant social and political life in a purpose-built modern city, to build not so much a garden city as a Social City.[7]

The speculative architect/builders of Georgian Bath tackled the same problem. By building terraced houses with unified facades they created a townscape of great order and rationality, but they gave their individual clients freedom to choose their own interiors. So they created an architecture which embodied public order *and* private freedom.

In his theological work, *The Meaning of the City*, Jacques Ellul is preoccupied with this same tension – between the penchant of city builders for order and the potential of the city for challenge. He concludes that in the Bible the city is the chief environmental strategy of a self-contained humanity which desired to exclude the challenge of a transcendent God. The city protected the Israelites not only from the vagaries of nature but also, they felt, from the piercing eye of their God. Solomon even built a town house for God – the temple at Jerusalem – to make sure that he was kept within human walls. God could not be contained, though, and it was in this same city that he chose to challenge his people in the person of Jesus.

Trees have also possessed an ambiguous symbolism throughout history. On the one hand, the tree symbolizes rootedness and security. Its roots mingle deeply with that primordial symbol of order, the earth; its branches provide shelter; and wood is a good, solid building material. Yet at the same time the branches of a tree spread outwards to the open air, the very opposite of the enclosed space of human dwellings. No human beings have yet been able to build structures that begin to approach the openness and outward-looking character of the tree. So trees have often been used to symbolize life and openness.

The tension between order and freedom, and its physical expression in place versus space, home versus travel, is the central theme in Kenneth Grahame's children's classic *The Wind in the Willows*. Homeloving chapters (such as 'The River Bank', 'Mr Badger', and 'Dulce Domum') are interrupted by chapters of adventure, exploration and travel (most notably the adventures of Mr Toad, but also the Mole's adventure in 'The Wild Wood', the young otter's in 'The Piper at the Gates of Dawn'; even Ratty himself questions his domesticated existence and breaks out in 'Wayfarers All'). All these adventures come to nothing but disaster in the end, the folly of the space/travel/freedom theme is exposed, and in true English style the author comes down firmly on the side of home.

There is probably more of a feeling in the United States than in any other nation that individual freedom and social order can go hand in hand. There is a strong sense that the American social order is based on individual freedom, and this is reflected in the way space, the big outdoors, is exalted. The vastnesses of prairie, desert and wilderness occupy an important place in the national mythology; the States are one of the few modern nations (Australia would be another) in which open space has become a national symbol in preference to enclosed place. The Grand Canyon, rather than being seen as a geological freak, is seen as typically American. (Typical symbols of English nation-hood, by contrast, are the thatched cottage and the enclosed field.) The national bird of the USA, the eagle, also symbolizes freedom. An American *Wind in the Willows* would favour the virtues of exploration and personal freedom over those of home and social order.

Not that Americans are without symbols of home. The log cabin and the old-timer rocking in his chair on his Mississippi front porch represent the home-spun virtues of old time family life, and are almost as powerful symbols as the prairie and its open skies. The two themes are jointly and thoroughly explored in Country and Western music: on the one hand the freedom of the travelling man and the cowboy, on the other the rural matriarch, source of every Christian and homely virtue.

People usually try to create an environment which contains both space and place, movement and stability, and which rep-resents freedom as well as order. Thus the British husband and wife who value car as well as house; the couple who enjoy 'going out' some evenings as much as 'staying in' on others; the sur-burbanite who enjoys hill-walking or back-packing for his fort-night's annual holiday. Often the balance is achieved through a sexual division of labour: the man travels far from home and is the representative of freedom, the woman tends the nest and is the symbol of order, her womb the symbol of security. (Earth and Nature are both female.)

Jay Appleton's book *The Experience of Landscape*[8] is a rare and brave attempt to provide a general answer to the questions 'what do we like about the landscape and why?'. His approach is inter-disciplinary and he rightly criticizes aesthetics for trying to reduce the question to a matter of whether a landscape is beautiful. Appleton shows that landscape is always seen by the human mind either as something protective and womb-like or as something open, which the human eye can roam over freely, or a combination of the two. He explains this combination of 'refuge' and 'prospect' in terms of evolution. Originally a hunting species, our prime environmental need as the hunter (or indeed as the hunted) was *to see but not be seen*, to command a prospect while being located in a refuge.

It may well be that prospect and refuge *are* dominant themes in the way human beings in western cultures perceive landscape. I have suggested in this chapter, however, that this may equally be accounted for in terms of the need for both freedom and security. To return once again to landscape paintings. Many depict vistas from relatively sheltered stances, a fact which may have much to do with our need for an environment which we can explore and grasp in the mind's eye while maintaining contact with base. We desire a world which is secure yet not closed, orderly yet free, and in which we can therefore feel at home.

Appleton's theory explicitly assumes that human perception rests on our biological heritage from those days, far back in human history though not in the time-scale of biological evolution, when man-the-hunter had to orient himself to the environment in a particular way if he was to survive. The logical gap between that and the finer points of a seventeenth-century Dutch landscape painting or the contemporary penchant for hill-walking is bridged only on the assumption that biology is primary. He provides no evidence of *how* this biological heritage actually affects the painter and the hill walker.

My view, expressed not only in this chapter but throughout the book, stresses the importance of ultimate beliefs and of religion in human affairs. I look at humans as spiritual as well as biological beings. No-one could very well deny the general importance of either religion or biology in human life, but what I have tried to show specifically is *how* people's religious needs and ultimate beliefs affect their dealings with environment, and *how* people strive to materialize their spiritual ideals in their environment. I have tried to show that it is not a big jump from the words of painters, mountaineers, planners, architects, housewives, landscape gardeners or tourists to my theory. The jump to Appleton's primeval man-the-hunter seems to me to be unacceptably huge. But the reader must decide for himself.

Chapter Eleven

ENVIRONMENTAL FEAR

'Anxiety strives to become fear, because fear can
be met by courage.'
Paul Tillich, The Courage To Be

If the environment is constructed physically and construed mentally as a home fit for humans, there always lurks the anxiety that it may turn out to be a less than perfect residence. The sense of being at home in the world is so essential for human well-being that this anxiety runs very deep – so deep that it is rarely recognized. Anxiety is non-specific fear; it cannot be endured for more than a moment, for it points to the meaninglessness of life, to our mortality or to our guilt. Perhaps the things we hold to be sacred and which hold our lives together are false? The thought is intolerable.

We cope with anxiety by converting it into specific fears, by projecting it onto specific objects, specific places and specific people. It is easy to be courageous against specific things and people, for they are finite enemies who can be resisted or avoided one at a time. The retired English colonel's anxiety that the whole world is going to the dogs is focused upon the heavy trucks thundering through his village; the American wife's anxiety about her marriage focuses on the belief that they are living in the wrong house, with the wrong associations, in the wrong neighbourhood, and if only they moved house then they would be able to make a fresh start.

In this chapter I will look at some ways in which anxiety is displaced onto the environment, and at how certain environments attract anxiety.

Terror on the roads

Death is the ultimate anxiety. Perhaps it has not always been, but it certainly is so in an individualistic society in which the all-too-mortal individual is of ultimate importance, rather than the more permanent entity of the tribe. Often it is the death of a loved one, spouse or child, rather than one's own death, which threatens to take all meaning out of life. At the same time, there is a taboo on talking about death, not so much in the States but certainly in Britain. The question arises, how do people cope with this anxiety which they have few opportunities to express?

By far the most common causes of death through the ages have come not from the human body wearing out of its own accord, but from the external environment. A common myth says that the tremendous decrease in mortality rates in the developed world in the last century or so has been the result of modern medicine and doctors' increasing ability to cure illnesses. In fact it has been due largely to public health measures: pure water, good housing, adequate food, smokeless zones and so on. And today, the main contributory factors to death have to do with lifestyles which introduce into the body unhealthy substances such as cigarettes, alcohol or too much food, together with environmental factors external to the body such as war, poor harvests, polluted workplaces and accidents.

Given that so many tangible, external things are the cause of death, one might expect anxiety about death to find expression in specific fears about places and objects known to contribute to mortality. Well, in fact one does not generally find people urging their loved ones to give up smoking, drinking or overeating, possibly because the link between these things and dying is not visible. The link is something which is to most people rather unreal, a scientific hypothesis. But there is one cause of death whose environmental cause is very clear, and that is the traffic accident. But even here, this does not lead to the general conclusion that roads are dangerous places, except in one important instance, which I would like to focus on now.

The group of people for whom most fear is expressed concerning the road is children. In one study in the United States, parents were asked what places they did not allow their children to go to and why; the biggest single response by far concerned traffic danger. The authors add that 'in general, the environmental fear of many parents seems out of proportion to statistical reality'.[1] I suspect that what leads to exaggerated fears for the safety of children is the general anxiety parents in a post-Freudian world have about their children. We believe that so much can go wrong at an early age which will mar a person for life, we attach an unprecedented importance to the bringing up of children, yet we are probably less trained for it than ever before. This is because in the small isolated family of today, the first baby a girl has to look after is likely to be her own and she is expected to be totally responsible for it. General anxiety about whether the child is safe (both emotionally and physically) finds expression in exaggerated fears about particular places and objects. The mother may have a fixation about electric sockets, stoves or a hundred and one other dangerous objects, but the place that she is systematically encouraged to fear is the road. Advertisements play on, and hence exacerbate, this fear.

One advert on British television shows a young mum going out to pay the milkman; she leaves the door ajar; the dog runs out after her; the child runs after the dog into the road, and in a horrifying climax is run over by a car whose vision was obscured by the milk van. There follows the caption: 'Make sure the under-fives stay inside'. The advert is saying that the roads spell such unmitigated terror, that the under-fives together with their mums (nearly a sixth of the population) should literally be locked inside. If such drastic curtailment of activity were imposed on any other sector of the population because of the fear of random death arising from simply going out, we would label the perpetrators of death as terrorists or terrorizers (as when people are afraid to go out at night because of the fear of mugging, or in a curfew during civil troubles). As far as the pre-school child is concerned, this advert is saying that the motor car driver should be avoided by means normally reserved as defences against terrorism or civil war.

This was explicitly recognized in the very early days of the motor car when it was not allowed to proceed at more than walking pace and had to be preceded by a man with a red flag. We have now come to accept cars, and place motorists' rights more highly than pedestrians'. (Highway authorities are much more concerned with traffic flow and the convenience of motorists than with pedestrians.) For the child who is too young to have learnt the despised and difficult role of pedestrian, the result is that the road becomes a place of terror. I suspect that future centuries may view the restrictions we place on children as a result of the motor car in the same way that we now consider the swaddling of children in olden days – barbaric and inhumane. A few years ago multi-storey flats went out of public favour for young families partly because the under-fives hardly ever got out. What was overlooked was that, if one goes by the book, they are not even allowed out of one or two-storey dwellings.

The problem derives from the combination of three things. One, in our society, children are deemed very precious. Child mortality, once the most common form of death, is now very rare; we feel outraged and cheated if our child should die. If life is sacred, the life of a child is doubly so.

Two, because children are seen as special, childhood has become a special time. Infants and toddlers have always been seen as categorically different from adults, but many societies have viewed children above the age of four or five as small adults who were expected, within their limits, to participate in the family economy. They would play their part in housework, weaving, harvesting, and so on. The idea that all pre-adolescent children are categorically different from adults and inhabit a categorically different world called 'childhood' is a rather recent idea. Childhood is a state in which play, spontaneity, games, and exploration are expected. One consequence of this is that children need to occupy a special physical environment – the playroom, playground or playschool – in which these decidely non-adult activities can be carried out safely, without interrupting the more important daily round of the adults.

Three; unfortunately, not all of childhood can be spent in such play areas. The child actually spends most of its time in environments built for and by adults. In particular, the child has to go across streets and roads; here he is unreasonably expected to abandon temporarily the joyous life of spontaneity and play-fulness which otherwise society has decreed sacred to his child-hood. Children have to cross roads on their own long before they have arrived at an age (about ten or twelve) when they are conceptually and physiologically equipped to do this in complete safety. It is not surprising that they are often bemused. One highly intelligent seven-year-old girl, well-trained by her parents in road sense, was asked how she managed when she wanted to cross the roadway. She replied: 'Well, you see, first I look to the right and then to the left and then to the right again. Then I stand there shaking – and then I run.'[2]

The road is a symbol of a contradiction: our complex tech-nological society holds sacred the simplicity and innocence of childhood, yet that precious thing called childhood has to exist in a totally unsuitable and dangerous context. The environment which reflects and embodies many of our cultural values (for example, our individualism) does not reflect the esteem in which we claim to hold childhood. Environment and culture are out of step, and not unnaturally this induces anxiety among parents.

Paradoxically, this anxiety can be turned to the advantage of the motor car, for it is the car that solves the problem of how to transport the child when he does have to go outside the house. Consider the following advert for Volvo estate cars in which this veritable tank of a vehicle is pictured next to a proud mum with her decidely naughty-looking yet adorable little boy on his first day to school. The caption goes:

'EVEN WHEN IT'S HALF EMPTY, IT TAKES A LOAD OFF YOUR MIND.

'To read most estate car advertisements you'd think the roads were full of people rushing six foot sofas from one side of the country to the other.

'In fact, most estate cars are used to carrying smaller, more fragile items.

'Like children . . .'

The advert goes on to describe the Volvo's many safety features.

'There are now five versions.
'All of them will take a six foot sofa with ease.
And a six-year-old child with safety.
'VOLVO. A CAR WITH STANDARDS.'

The advert contrasts the preciousness of the modern child with the danger of the modern road, and claims that the Volvo is the only sure answer. It is saying that it takes at least £7000/$15,000 (1980 prices) to take a child anywhere near a public road.

In the 1950s and early 60s when I was a schoolboy we mostly walked, cycled or took a bus or train to school. Today the morning rush hour traffic jams in many towns are caused in large part by children being chauffeured to school in private cars. A vicious circle is being set up: the roads are becoming more crowded, and therefore more dangerous; so more people go by car than bicycle – I know of adults who do not bicycle in certain parts of town because of the traffic danger; so the roads become more crowded. Fear produces the very thing that causes the fear.

Chauffeuring of children also encourages the 'voyeur' view of the world which I described in my earlier discussions of sight-seeing and of landscape as art. Walking entails a multi-sensa-tional encounter with the world, meeting all kinds of people and animals and curious objects as one goes. Being chauffeured forces one to look out at the world through a protective pane of glass. The world becomes defined as a visual object, and the speed of the car means that you cannot look at any one place for more than a few moments. If chauffeuring children is in-tended to keep them alive, then the life it is preparing them for is that of a tourist. Censorious parents who disapprove of the effect of television on children for precisely this reason do not seem to realize that driving them around in their Volvos may produce much the same effect.

The sublime and the terrible
Strange to say, the places which induce terror when there is real, or really imagined, danger of death can take on an alto-gether different quality when we know that we ourselves are not

endangered. Part of the fascination of watching rock climbing, motor racing and other apparently dangerous sports is that for non-participants they provide a ritualized glimpse into death, by displaying people facing death with equanimity, and thereby may help the spectator to come to terms with his own feelings about death. One's heart misses a beat as the television shows the climber fall or the racing cars touch, and thereby the spectators express their anxiety about death, even if only to themselves.

This vicarious experience is not new. It was a basic component in Edmund Burke's philosophical treatise on *The Sublime and the Beautiful*. Two hundred years ago, Burke wrote:

'When danger or pain press too nearly, they are incapable of giving any delight, and are simply terrible; but at certain distances, and with certain modifications, they may be, and they are delightful, as we every day experience . . . Pain and danger are simply painful when their cause actually affect us; they are delightful when we have an idea of pain and danger, without being actually in such circumstances; this delight I have not called pleasure, because it turns on pain, and because it is different enough from any idea of positive pleasure. Whatever excites this delight, I call sublime.'

And, writing 2,000 years ago, the Latin poet Lucretius described this same experience, without Burke's tiresome jargon:

'Sweet it is, when on the great sea the winds are buffeting the waters, to gaze from the land on another's great struggles; not because it is pleasure or joy that any one should be distressed, but because it is sweet to perceive from what misfortune you yourself are free.'

I imagine that many a modern tourist gazing up at the climbers on the Eiger or the cliffs of Yosemite feels much the same.

As our reaction to such places switches from fear to awe, so the place itself changes from being terrible to being sublime. Early commentators on the industrial revolution noted how the unprecedented power of the new steam engines had this ability to appear one moment terrible, the next sublime. Perhaps there is something of this too in the modern motor car, and no-one would be more aware of this than the police: one moment they are throbbing down the motorway at 100 mph in their elegant machines in the pursuit of justice, the next they are attending the child who has been knocked over by just such a machine.

The diseased body

One of the most fundamental prerequisites for human well-being is that one feels at home in one's own body. This is perhaps a particular problem in western societies in which we are continually bombarded with idealized images of the perfect male and female bodies, which our actual bodies can never match up to (see chapter two). Even apart from any fear of death, sickness poses a particular threat. Physical pain can be so preoccupying that it sours one's whole being: the grumpy old man most likely has internal ailments of one kind or another.

How then do we think of pain and sickness? In non-western societies there are three common views about disease. *Object intrusion* – some alien body has entered the body; *spirit invasion* – the sick person has had a curse placed on him or her; *soul loss* – the person is sick because he has transgressed some taboo. Western medicine has opted almost exclusively for the first: sickness involves intrusion into the body by alien objects, which we call germs. Even when germs are not accounted responsible, as for example with a broken leg, the sickness is still seen as something external: thus 'I *have* a broken leg', not 'I *am* a broken leg', just as 'I've got a cold' or 'I've caught a cold' rather than 'I'm cold'.

Most of the time we count our bodies as part of ourselves, in contrast to the external environment. So one way of being at ease with ourselves when we are ill is to see the illness not as part of our bodies but as something from the external environment which has temporarily and illegitimately invaded us. In effect, we repeat an old trick of politicians: claiming credit for ourselves when things are going well, and blaming someone or something else when things go badly. It is certainly a time-honoured way of keeping one's end up. We make the sick body, or at least the sick part of it, into an 'it' rather than a part of 'me'.

We often conceive of internal organs, even when healthy, as objects, and we are quite happy talking about *the* heart, or *the* appendix, rather than *my* heart or *my* appendix. With external organs we usually only do this when we are ill. Thus 'Take *my* hand, darling' ('the hand' would be inexcusable here), but 'It's *the* right hand that's got the pain, doctor'. This way of talking does not just come from doctors who are trained as scientists and therefore to deal with objects not people. It comes, if anything even more so, from patients. Patients need to reassure themselves that illness is not random and that bodies do not simply wear out, for this would mean that the universe was too disturbing and disorderly to be part of; they want an explanation, preferably one which locates the cause somewhere outside of themselves.

This also perhaps goes some way to explain many people's resistance to holistic or psychosomatic explanations of illness. These explanations – modern equivalents of 'soul loss' and 'spirit invasion' – identify the illness as a result of the person's lifestyle (smoking, drinking, over-eating), or as part and parcel of his emotional problems and his relations with others. Such approaches say that the whole psyche is sick, which is more than most people want to know.

This raises the interesting question of why some illnesses *are* talked of as characterizing the whole person in addition to being an invasion by an outside 'it'. This way of talking is typically used of someone else, not of oneself. Thus 'he *is* a leper/epileptic/arthritic' as well as 'he *has* leprosy/epilepsy/arthritis'. I do not see what makes such diseases different from others, but what is clear is why the sufferers of such diseases would rather say 'I suffer from epilepsy' than 'I *am* an epileptic'. They do not want to be defined by their disease. The ultimate social disaster is for it to be known that you *are* a leper; you certainly cannot be at home in the world if that is how people see you.

Most people, if they are lucky, get only one illness at a time, and it is easy to objectify and externalize each complaint as it arises. In later years, though, the ailments may come piling up several at a time. At first, the person responds as follows: 'I'm basically in good health, it's just my leg'. To this is then added, 'It's just my liver/memory/hearing', until the list becomes so long that it is not possible to carry on maintaining that one is in good health. This can be a worrying and disturbing time for probably one is not ill, in the sense of being in bed or in hospital. The only possible way of making sense of it all is to admit that one is growing old and that one's body is wearing out. 'I have arthritis' becomes 'I am arthritic'. At this point, the swearing at bits of one's body for not keeping up to scratch may well diminish, and a new reconciliation with oneself ensue.

The loss of control

One of the worrying things about an ageing body is that it is no longer as much under our control as we would like. Certainly those diseases in which limbs do not obey the will's commands are most disturbing. In this section I want to look a little at what it is like living in an environment which one cannot control.

In the previous chapter I described how the city and the street provide spaces away from the observation of elders and betters, where the youngster is consequently freer to behave as *he* desires rather than as others desire. But the other side of the coin is that those very eyes which the youngster is escaping can be worried sick about what their offspring are up to while out of sight. They are anxious about the freedom which urban spaces provide for their children.

Some years ago when I was doing some research on delinquency, one thing which came across very consistently was what parents held to be the cause for their children getting into trouble. Social work agencies largely held the parents to blame, along with a host of subsidiary factors such as poor housing, bad schools, the local subculture and the neighbourhood. Parents clearly saw the blame to be with the other kids that their boy hung around with. It was the street not the home that they considered the dangerous place. In answer to the question 'In what ways did he worry you at home?', parents talked most frequently of activities *outside* the home:[3]

'Pals he kept,'
'Staying away from home,'
'Not going to school,'
'We lived in a rough area, he got in with rough
boys and started getting in trouble rather than be
made fun of. He is very easily led.'

Given that most juvenile offences are committed outside the home, the parents' explanation in terms of the social dynamics of the street demands to be taken as seriously as supposedly more sophisticated explanations to do with family dynamics or Oedipus complexes. If the street is where the child meets his compatriots in crime and where they commit their offences, it is certainly not unreasonable for parents to see the street as a danger area.[4]

Academic support for the parents' view has come from Oscar Newman in his architectural book *Defensible Space*. He shows how the local lower working class street used to act as a buffer between the private world of the home and the anonymous public world of the city. The street and the neighbourhood provided a communal area; people felt some responsibility for it and they would do something to defuse trouble if trouble was brewing. And certainly they would defend it against intruders. In high-rise apartment blocks, Newman argues, this defensible intermediate space is all but non-existent. The front door of the apartment marks a boundary between the private home and the anonymous stair or corridor. Strangers can wander around unnoticed within the apartment block in a way they could not in the older neighbourhoods. Once out of the front door, children are beyond external control and their good behaviour is entirely dependent on internal control provided by their own strength of character. The peculiarly modern problem is not, as many believe, the lack of control within families, but the lack of control in the street.

This provides the context in which mugging has become a public issue. In point of fact people are not very likely to be mugged, as Celia Fremlin has shown in her moving experiment of wandering the streets of London alone at night. A heart attack in bed or an automobile accident are far more likely than a brutal attack by a stranger. But the very thought of attack produces enormous anxiety in women. Rather than go through the painful business of revising the romantic concept of feminity, which lies at the heart of women feeling defenceless and attackers assuming them to be, it is much easier for them to project this anxiety onto the street, in particular the street at night, and simply to avoid such places.

This is not to say that fear of the darkened street is a uniquely modern or feminine problem. In the late eighteenth century, before police forces were rationalized and street gas lights were introduced, in general no one went out at night for fear of being attacked and robbed. Rural roads, even in daylight, carried the danger of highwaymen. Then, as now, the fear derived from being in a place where one was not sure that one was in control of events. This is the exact opposite of that mastery of the environment, of being in control of events, which is so powerful an ideal in western societies today. The fear that one may not have this mastery is deeply disturbing, quite apart from any physical threat to life and limb.

This perhaps lies at the root of the fear of open spaces which many people experience. This need not be a pathological agoraphobia which drastically curtails a person's way of life, but simply a sense of disorientation in wide open spaces. Some people, especially those from more intimate urban or rural landscapes, find the desert or the vast featureless prairies of the American west rather disturbing. Here are environments which are difficult to relate to, and certainly to feel at home in.

For others, the modern megalopolis has much the same effect. Walking not only gets you nowhere fast but also emphasizes your insignificance in relation to the vast, soulless urban scene. Some may enjoy walking through Manhattan for the sense of awe they feel there, but few urban scenes are dramatic enough to induce this religious, aesthetic sensation.

The automobile and other forms of transport help to restore the sense of scale between the traveller and the urban scene, and help him feel at home in it:

'One of the strongest visual sensations is a relation
of scale between an observer and a large
environment, a feeling of adequacy when
confronted by a vast space: that even in the midst
of such a world one is big enough, powerful
enough, identifiable enough. In this regard, the
automobile, with its speed and personal control,
may be a way of establishing such a sense at a new
level. At the very least, it begins to neutralize the
disparity in size between a man and a city.'[5]

This goes some way to explaining why it is that in America, with its vast cities and continental expanses, people feel so at home in the automobile. The motorist is akin to the skier who is able to relate to a vast, featureless landscape which would terrify the pedestrian:

'The sense of personal mastery of space is
strongest on skis or on a motor-cycle, where the
vehicle is small and delicately controlled, where
one is "outside" in contact with the environment,
and where it is impossible to make body motions
within the vehicle which are irrelevant to the
motion through the landscape. The sense of
mastery is the product of both manoeuverable
velocity and a sensuous contact . . .
'Particularly if the road swings smoothly from
point to point of a fine and rather open natural
landscape, it gives the same sense of vital rhythm
and movement as a skier's track.'[6]

In my experience the attraction of sports such as ski-ing,

dinghy sailing and mountain climbing is not that one is in total and unassailable control of the environment, but that one is in provisional control. One always has to be alert to the environment reasserting supremacy, and there is pleasure at being *just* in control. Dinghy racing is far more exhilarating in conditions where without the finest balance of body and dinghy a capsize will result than in tamer conditions, for the balance between body and environment is brought to a high pitch. Similarly, in mountain climbing accurate map reading and weather forecasting are critical; whereas in walking they are merely useful. In tame conditions, one merely wanders through the landscape or seascape, unaware of the surroundings except at those odd moments when one chooses to contemplate them aesthetically. Sailing or climbing at the limit means being continuously aware of one's surroundings which can be uniquely exhilarating.

Awe or terror?

Some of the more mystically inclined do enjoy spaces whose very formlessness terrifies others. The American conservationist Robert Marshall, in a classic article on the value of the wilderness, wrote:

'Any one who has looked across a ghostly valley at
midnight, when moonlight makes a formless silver
unity out of the drifting fog, knows how impossible
it often is in nature to distinguish mass from
hallucination. Any one who has stood upon a lofty
summit and gazed over an inchoate tangle of deep
canyons and cragged mountains, of sunlit lakes
and black expanses of forest, has become aware of
a certain giddy sensation that there are no
distances, no measures, simply unrelated matter
rising and falling without any analogy to the banal
geometry of breadth, thickness and height.'[7]

Such ungraspable formlessness can be experienced either with terror or with sublime appreciation. Those places which defy human control, which defy even the ability of eye and brain to organize them into a coherent pattern, are typically seen with deep feeling, either for or against. The oceans, the high mountains, the wilderness, have always been seen as either places of terror, or places of beauty.

Normally, we have little difficulty in categorizing what we see in the world around us: that red blob is a combine harvester and is in the field half a mile away; that bright point is a star, probably some millions of light-years away; that darkening of the sky is a cloud which may soon mean rain. Simple categories such as agriculture, astronomy and meteorology enable us to make sense of what we see. We can judge distance and brightness easily once we have classified an object into such categories: we see the star as brighter than a nearby street lamp (which is in fact producing many more lumens) because we know that it is an astronomical phenomenon, infinitely further away.

Occasionally, though, our categories do not seem to work, and in consequence we cannot grasp or mentally control our sensations. This may produce *fear*, as in a bad trip on hallucinogenic drugs, or it may induce *awe*.

I have experienced sheer, naked awe only once, and it is significant that the other person present experienced fear. The occasion was a particularly spectacular and unexpected display in Northern Scotland of the aurora borealis, or 'northern lights'. In Britain, these are usually confined to a minor display above the northern horizon, and one views them with curiosity from the outside, rather as one does an unusual picture or view. Once one has satisfied one's curiosity, one may then turn to other matters. This particular display, however, consisted of shafts of coloured light and blimps of moving silvery light coming up from the full 360 degrees of the horizon, converging at the top of the heavens in a fiery red pattern. It lit the landscape with the brightness of a full moon, but as the light came from the whole sky, there were no shadows. There was no escaping it; you could not look the other way, for it contained the entire heavens and it continued for hours. You *had* to make sense of it. And the problem, I concluded afterwards, was that I could *not* make sense of it. Intuition told us that events of that brightness in the night sky must come within the category of astronomy rather than earth-bound meteorology, yet if all this *was* happening on the astronomical scale millions of miles away then surely the universe was going mad. In fact, aurorae occur in the upper atmosphere between the levels of earth-bound weather and astronomical phenomena. This was what induced the anxiety and the awe, for we have little or no concept of this intermediary level. In more northern climes where aurorae of this magnificence are common, they no longer induce these reactions; they are probably accepted as being in a category of their own. In Scotland, however, it was a strange experience.

Some people experience thunder and lightning with awe or fear. Lightning in particular crosses the fundamental boundaries of night and day, heaven and earth, hot (lightning) and cold (rain). I guess that this puzzlement over categories is what makes young children fascinated with lakes, rivers and puddles (for how can water lie on land?), with snow (for how can solids come out of the sky?) and with ice (for how can liquid be solid?). Until the categories are sorted out, one cannot be at ease in the world.

Anxiety and the American landscape

In the previous chapter, I mentioned the positive value placed in the United States on freedom and personal mobility. This has helped create a landscape that sometimes, however, hints at something most of us would rather not know about: the frailty of the human condition.

To my European eyes, the typical American house appears somehow transitory (which need not detract from its beauty; if anything the reverse). It is built of less durable materials than its British counterpart, wood instead of brick. One can somehow imagine both its construction and its eventual demolition. Dust to dust, like humans. One is not surprised to come across ghost towns in America, because one can somehow imagine every town having a beginning and an end (perhaps the same is true in Australia). There is something poignant about a home, which should emanate warmth and security, reminding one of transitoriness and eventual emptiness.

This is what I find moving about the houses painted by Andrew Wyeth. To Americans his paintings connote the old homely virtues, very New England and very settled. But to my European eye, his houses have a certain sadness and loneliness that is very American. They seem empty, abandoned, having been inhabited for only a few years. A home should be full of children and laughter, the continuity of the generations, but there is rarely more than an isolated individual in Wyeth's houses. One finds this same lonely abandonment in Woody Allen's evocative film *Interiors* in which the characters temporarily inhabit a virtually empty summer house in isolation by the sea.

Of course, one finds ghost towns and derelict houses in other countries. The Scottish highlands are liberally sprinkled with crofters' cottages abandoned in the Clearances of the late nineteenth century when the crofters were evicted from their land. These are houses with no future, but they do have the feel of a long past, and they have a romantic attraction as a result. Wyeth's houses not only have no future, they have no past either. They are the temporary resting places of the man or the woman or the child on the move.

The poignancy of Wyeth's houses is that they hint at something deeper still; the potential homelessness of all human beings. They hint at the possibility that, after all, we have no viable place in the cosmos; the possibility that, like Cain, we are permanent wanderers on the Earth, struggling to create a home for ourselves. Wyeth's paintings, for me, reveal the fragility of the homes we create for ourselves, or at least that Americans create for themselves.

It may not be insignificant that it is *American* intellectuals who have developed the idea of ourselves as homeless – sociologists such as Peter Berger, theologians such as Walter Brueggemann. Precisely because of the difficulty Americans find in staying in one place, they may be peculiarly aware of the frailty inherent in the human condition of us all. They intuitively feel that we are all wanderers, struggling to make a meaningful place out of meaningless space. Socially and physically rootless, they can see better than most the spiritual homelessness of all of us. They find it more difficult than most to create landscapes and homes that completely cover up this homelessness.

Chapter Twelve

WHAT CAN WE DO WITH THE SPIRITS IN THE FOREST?

'The intelligibles which our intellect understands
are derived from sensibles.'

Thomas Aquinas, *Contra Gentiles*

In this book I have tried to show that the physical environment
is not just the source of tangible things such as shelter, food,
energy and raw materials, hurricanes, pollution and starvation.
Much more than this, people make their environment symbolize
less tangible things; in contemporary society, for example, environments have been made to symbolize freedom, status, power
and order, and to provide non-physical properties such as privacy. These properties are highly valued because they are close
to people's ultimate concerns such as their belief in the sanctity
of the individual and the assured hope in progress. Only when
the tangible environment matches up with a people's ultimate
beliefs – their shared religion (however implicit and secular that
may be) – can they feel at home in the world.

It seems to me that this understanding of the religious nature
of even our supposedly secular contemporary world is the key
to bringing together the wide and varied research on landscape
perception and environmental psychology which has proliferated
in the 1970s. So far the researchers have produced many isolated
nuggets of insight (I think especially of the humanistic geographers Yi-Fu Tuan and David Lowenthal) but no coherent philosophical framework into which the nuggets may be inserted to
build a worthy edifice.

I have tried to lay the foundations for such an edifice by

producing evidence that people symbolize their physical surroundings in ways, and for purposes, which are essentially religious. Some readers may not agree that the evidence warrants
this conclusion, and here they must part company with me. In
this final chapter I want to address those who *do* think the
evidence warrants the conclusion. The question I wish to ask
them is this: is it desirable that human beings *should* inject
religious meaning into their physical surroundings? I will consider three possible answers to this question. They doubtless do
not exhaust the possible answers and, though logically each
excludes the other, in practice many readers (and indeed myself
also) may often adopt some uneasy synthesis between two or
more of them.

Functionalism

One response is to accept that the use of the environment for
religious and symbolic purposes as described in this book is
simply the way things are and must be accepted as inevitable.
The question as to whether it is desirable is a non-question, in
this view. This seems to be the view of most humanist
geographers.

Religious ideas and abstract human ideals have always required some kind of manifestation, some kind of embodiment
in physical symbols which make tangible the intangible.
Religions have always had their idols and their icons which make
the presence of the deity visible. Attempts at creating a purely
spiritual religion with no such physical symbols have always
failed. The redecoration of English churches during the Reformation provide just one example: no sooner had the old medieval religious wall paintings been condemned as idolatrous and
whitewashed over than the royal coat of arms was erected in
their place.

Much the same is true of modern secular abstract ideals such
as freedom. Without visible and symbolic embodiment they
would be difficult to grasp. Such was the view put forward by
one proponent of the New England Heritage Trail in Boston,
who argued that the trail would present

'visual, living, documented proof . . . in brick and
stone, in hill and square and heights and halls . . .
that freedom was for the American people always
in the inner soul of their being.'[1]

Those who are fortunate enough to believe in the particular
values which are embodied in their environment are as happy
with this state of affairs as the medieval priest with his wall
paintings, for they make his abstract ideals real to other people.

This use of the tangible to represent the intangible is in fact
the only way in which we can talk of abstract matters. In his
discussion of metaphor C. S. Lewis noted that

'Anyone who talks about things that cannot be
seen, or touched, or heard, or the like, must
inevitably talk *as if they could be* seen or touched
or heard (for example must talk of 'complexes'
and 'repressions' *as if* desires could really be tied
up in bundles or shoved back; or 'growth' and
'development' *as if* institutions could really grow
like trees or unfold like flowers; of energy being
'released' *as if* it were an animal let out of a
cage).'[2]

Likewise, poetry uses material images to express difficult ideas
or emotional states; and how else can children learn a language
if they do not build up their vocabulary from the tangible and
then move from there onto more abstract concepts? The nuclear
physicist may describe molecular goings on in the language of
mathematics, but he also needs images and models from the
visible, tangible everyday world; certainly his pupils cannot do
without such models before graduating to mathematical
concepts.

So the symbolic use of the environment is *functional* for us
human beings, and we cannot do without it.

It is possible to be quite cynical and pragmatic about this,
believing that it matters little whether the abstract ideas represented in the environment are *true* or not. If the ideas and their

material representations give shape to life, if they enable children to talk and pupils to understand physics, if they provide some comfort to the medieval peasant and if they generally make us at ease in the world, then they are useful and therefore valid. In a pragmatic society, in which human happiness is valued more highly than truth, what matters is whether we feel at home in the world, not whether the world we imagine ourselves to inhabit is actually the real world.

Leo Marx has made a classic and invaluable study of images of landscape in American literature. In a subsequent article on this 'pastoral' genre of American literature he has drawn out the implications of his study for contemporary planning. In this article he displayed an unashamed functionalism. His studies had demonstrated that Americans hold (and have held for many years) three distinct images of the landscape – the settled community of city and town; productive farmland; and untamed wilderness – and his studies had demonstrated that these three images form a major part of American culture and of the American psyche. His article goes on to conclude that therefore these images should be encouraged. The unstated logic is that because the images perform certain functions, therefore they are good. Functions become needs. That which exists becomes that which we cannot do without. 'Is' becomes 'ought':

'Another principle suggested by literary
pastoralism is the importance of diversity in
physical settings – the *need* to preserve the
distinctness of the three spheres of our
environment: the city, the rural countryside, and
the wilderness. Our literature supports the idea
that each of these performs an important role in
our psychic economy, and that . . . each offers
indispensable satisfactions. Hence the prospect of
the disappearance of any one of them, or of the
irrevocable blurring of the boundaries between
them, as in the spread of suburbia, *would be an
intolerable loss.*'[3] (My emphases.)

I am not interested here in whether we agree with Marx's conclusions (personally I do), but in the logic by which he arrives at them (which I find dubious).

This pragmatic functionalism is very common among planners and politicians. At the end of the day, they have to do what people want, and people manifestly do want to feel comfortable emotionally as well as physically. Thus Kevin Lynch, Professor of City Planning at the Massachusetts Institute of Technology says: 'A good environment gives its possessor an important sense of emotional security.' Architects and social scientists often pride themselves on being something of an élite, one step ahead of the common man or woman, yet they too tend to think that a functional environment is a good environment. The question of *which* values an environment represents is irrelevant in this view, so long as it makes people happy. The fact that the massive architecture of most repressive totalitarian regimes (for example, Ancient Rome's Coliseum or Moscow's Red Square) is also highly functional and provides members of such societies with a sense of emotional security seems to me to put a question mark over the view that what is functional is necessarily good.

Rationalism[4]

We come now to those responses which deny that the state of affairs described in this book is inevitable. A rationalist or secularist might hold that it is high time that human beings came of age and ceased to be concerned with fancy metaphysical problems such as where we fit in the universe, the meaning of life, and religion. And if people do want to tackle such complex and non-empirical ideas, they should certainly not drag the material world into their sophistries. Only things which are empirically demonstrable can be true or meaningful, so there is little point in discussing religion or the meaning of life. The material world, by contrast, can be talked of meaningfully, because it is tangible; it only muddies the issue if we make the material world represent fuzzy issues like religion and metaphysics.

In this materialist view, our material needs for shelter, food and so on are primary. Our relation to the environment should be a simple matter (and here rationalists differ among themselves) either of employing technology to exploit the environment efficiently for our material well-being; or of understanding the laws of ecology so that we may arrive at a long-term balance with the other species with whom we share this finite earth. Increasing our scientific knowledge, technological or ecological, is the means to these empirically necessary ends.

Rationalist materialism is the attitude found in some of those who are concerned about world poverty and overpopulation, and who would respond by limiting their own lifestyle for the sake of the world's poor. Decisions over material resources, they believe, should be based on the material needs of the human species. The fact that they find it hard to keep to such an ascetic program may be because they underestimate the symbolic and emotional functions provided by material goods and the material environment. Likewise, many of those who denounce the materialism of our consumer society fail to understand the ways in which material goods are valued as symbols rather than as material additions to personal wealth. Showing people that many of their consumer goods are 'luxuries' and that therefore they do not really need them, supposes that the only real needs are material needs. Which is materialism par excellence!

Rationalist materialism is where we began this book: rationalists call a spade a spade. This view has been influential in modern architecture in the fashion known as functionalism (nothing to do with the functionalism of the previous section). Reacting against the falsity of neo-classicism which made a civic hall look like a Greek temple and against the ornamentation of baroque architecture which made opera houses look like Christmas cakes, functionalist architects believed that the function of a building should be immediately apparent. A building should be what it looks like, and should look like what it is. Buildings should not have meanings injected into them which derive from anything outside the basic function of the building itself. This kind of architecture made a stand for truth at the expense of greatly limiting the meaning which a building could embody. There are real difficulties in actually living in an urban environment which is nakedly true but short on meaning, and this has much to do with the disfavour such architecture has recently fallen into.

Academics often see rationalism as the spirit of our age. Sociologist Max Weber saw rationality and bureaucracy becoming the keys to modern life, and some theologians (such as Harvey Cox) have likewise come to believe that rationality and pragmatism are what make modern people tick. There are no spirits left in the forests; forests are now simply so many million dollars' or pounds'-worth of realizable timber, or part of the resources donated by a fruitful planet for us to conserve. Similarly, Mircea Eliade thinks that the unified cosmos of traditional societies in which God, environment and culture are all of a piece is something which modern people have little experience or comprehension of. Modern society is desacralized: although there may still be traces of religion in the individual's private life and in his subconscious, we are subject to a process of secularization which seems inevitable.

Not all rationalism is materialist. There are those who would agree that even today people imbue their physical environment with sacred meaning, but would argue that this way of experiencing the environment is false. The task of the intellectual is to *demystify* the world, to strip people of the illusions which they cling to so dearly. Often such advocates of demystification have great sympathy for people's desire to live with an illusory image of the world, for the demystifiers fully realize the importance of such illusions for making ourselves at home in the world. Their dilemma is that on the one hand they appreciate the function of myths and symbols of sacredness, yet on the other they cannot tolerate their inherent falsity. A good example of this is Ann Oakley's sympathetic exposé of how the housewife sets standards for herself in housework which she then projects outside herself and believes to be sacred, objective, independent standards which demand to be kept up at all costs. The housewife imprisons herself, and acts as her own jailer.[5] The hope is that such exposés will liberate people from slavery to the myths which enslave them, without at the same time creating lives as devoid of meaning as those modernist buildings which the architects have stripped of meaning in the search for honesty.

The liberated person is one whose life is governed by a rational mind rather than by myths and mystifications.

Monotheism

A radical Christian or Jewish response would be that only God can provide salvation, and that human beings avoid this truth by seeking it in the material world about them. Only God is worthy of the worship which people today direct to idols such as Nature and the Individual, and salvation is to be found only through faith in this God, not through faith in human progress or in technology.

The material world is important because God created us as material beings, and so we can feel at home on the Earth. Nor is there any way we are justified in lording it over our fellow creatures, for we share with them a God-given creatureliness. The world is important also because it is the stage on which the drama of human history is enacted; it is given partly for human beings to explore and delight in. There is certainly a theological basis here for art, poetry, photography, science, gardening or any other human activity that opens up the richness of the created Earth.

But the Earth can provide no more than earthly benefits. The apostle Paul's teaching on marriage, often falsely maligned, simply pointed out that marriage meets some of our earthly needs, and should not be exalted as especially spiritual (teaching much needed in a romantic twentieth century that believes sex to be a spiritual act). Likewise, the physical environment is replete with meaning for us humans, and this is good. But the meaning is produced by us humans. It is not spiritual. Landscape can point to the spiritual, but can never itself be spiritual. The Psalmist wrote

'I lift up my eyes to the hills.
From whence does my help come?
My help comes from the Lord,
who made heaven and earth.'

His salvation came from God, not from the earth.

The problem comes when humanity rejects God and so has to look to the world to meet its spiritual needs. No longer can we rest in the knowledge that we are at home on the Earth; we have to *make* the Earth our home. Which is what this book has been all about.

The Genesis account of the fall describes Cain's lostness following the murder of his brother; this represents the condition shared by all human beings in their denial of God. Cain attempts to save himself by building himself a new environment: he builds a city, and he immerses himself in family life. Now he can forget that he is Cain the murderer, and live in an environment which reflects back to him the image of Cain the master-builder and proud father. From then onwards, the Bible describes with pity the efforts of human beings to create a city and an environment in which they can be self-sufficient; the story could be carried on into the present with the more utopian hopes of some architects and planners. Biblical religion rejects any claim that by building a new environment human beings can save themselves.

Nor can they save themselves by retreating into the loving arms of a created world which mankind has elevated to divine importance: Mother Nature. Vacations in the wilderness or lessons in ecology will not solve major human problems such as urban decay and violence, the arms race and starvation. These derive ultimately from the moral failings of human beings, such as hate, fear and selfishness and their political expression, which are part of the nature of fallen humanity. Mother Nature cannot change human nature.

So Christianity shares with rationalism the belief that there is nothing sacred about the material environment, and in this Christianity and rationalism are united against many other religions. Where Christianity and materialist rationalism differ is this: whereas Christianity claims that the physical world cannot be a source of spiritual fulfilment because this can only come from God, rationalism claims that the physical world cannot have spiritual power and meaning because such things simply do not exist.

Christianity shares with functionalism the understanding that people do need to have some central focus in their lives, something which provides meaning to existence, but it rejects functionalism's willingness to sacrifice truth in the search for meaning. For Christianity it is vitally important that what gives meaning to life should be *true*, that what we place at the centre of the universe truly is the centre of the universe.

Whereas functionalism opts for comfort and meaning at the expense of truth, and rationalism opts for truth at the expense of comfort, the good news claimed by Christianity is that both are possible when life centres around Jesus Christ. There is then no need to find ultimate meaning in the created world, for this is found in its creator. At the same time, the world is important because it is God's world. So our material and social environment is significant, but it is not the source of all significance. And understanding this frees people to rejoice in the world and to participate in it without being dependent on it.

Nevertheless, Christianity has had its own unfortunate brands of functionalism and rationalism. The medieval church surrounded the Christian with visual images and icons, and offered special shrines as the pilgrim's goal, all of which provided the comforting illusion that God's grace existed within the material world and could be touched and handled. Comforting, but untrue. Then there were the idol-smashing Puritans who saw through the illusion, but in their passion for truth left the believer with a physical environment which was colourless and comfortless.

At their best, however, the medievals and the puritans did grasp important truths. The medievals realized how people's physical surroundings, created by God, reflected much of that God. Objects and places were used in profusion to symbolize truths about God, and the whole world became a magnificent visual aid. The technical term for this was 'natural theology': nature as well as the Bible told people about God.

This follows the Biblical pattern of seeing the physical world as given by God, without itself being God. The Psalms of David are full of this, as are the parables of Jesus. Parables talk about tangible things which people are familiar with, in order to symbolize truths about God. Thus sheep and shepherds, rocks, kings, rich men, acorns and oak trees, all point beyond themselves to God. But the crucial thing about parables is that there is no possibility of confusing God with acorns, shepherds and the like. Parables clearly make the physical world out to be a pointer to the divine, but clearly distinguish it from the divine.

Some modern Christian writers, such as Michel Quoist in his *Prayers of Life*, still talk in parables. Quoist points to deep truths through such ordinary things as a wire fence, a blackboard, a brick or a telephone. His parables inject meaning into things and places, without denying that the meaning always remains provisional, always provided by us humans. Nobody could mistake a real fence for the fence which Quoist makes it symbolize, and nobody would idolize fences (as they have done mountains or the sky) simply because fences can point to deeper truths. This is because Quoist, like Jesus, takes simple, mundane things as his starting point. Nor does he take the superficial visual clichés of our culture – pandas, lion cubs, Mount Fiji – and try to give them Christian meaning, as do so many religious posters, and thereby trivialize religion by making it subservient to sentimentality. Not for him a world divided into sacred and profane, the meaningful and the meaningless, the colourful and the colourless.

Quoist's whole environment is rich with meaning, but he knows the meaning is always provisional, supplied by human beings, and so he does not deceive himself.

Parables are *a* way of talking, *a* way of seeing, and even the holiest saint does not talk in parables or see in parables for more than a tiny minority of the time. The richness and colour of the tangible world for the Christian does not depend on its being a pointer to God, but on the knowledge that it was given by God for us to use and enjoy. Though they did not fully appreciate how to rejoice in and enjoy the material world, the puritans did appreciate the world as a gift given by God for people to use. Having realized that there were no spirits or demons in the material world, they knew that there was nothing preventing them from exploring it fully through science and utilizing its resources through human industry. They enthusiastically entered the world in the enlightened understanding that there was nothing sacred about it – and thereby, for better or for worse, helped prepare the way for capitalism, for rationalism, and for our current ecological difficulties.

Protestants have been criticized for doing both too much and too little to their environment. On the one hand they are accused of abusing it rather than using it because they did not see it as sacred. On the other hand, they are supposed to have been too heavenly minded to be concerned about looking after the Earth. At the time of writing, for example, many environmental groups are claiming that the present development-minded American Secretary of State for the Interior, James Watt, has been given licence by his fundamentalist religion to exploit the American environment without concern for the future.

There may be more or less truth in these accusations against Watt and other biblical protestants through the centuries. What I want to make clear is that neglect of the Earth is not the inevitable conclusion to be drawn from biblical religion. The criticisms of ecology, of the worship of nature and the wilderness cult which I have made in this book can indeed lead to a right-wing development-minded interpretation: that once the absurdity of such cults has been exposed, we are free to move in and make as much money (and mess) as we like out of the de-frocked Earth. This is not my conclusion, though, and I cannot make this too clear.

I believe that once the absurdity of the belief that nature can save us has been revealed we are forced back to the true location of human problems. The human misery of the ghetto will not be solved by teaching the blacks the virtues of rural life but by political activity within the ghetto. The arms race will not be solved by lessons in ecology, but by the political courage of the people. Vacations in the wilderness provide only marginal relief for the overworked company executive who is the product of a whole system that needs changing. My criticism of most environmentalists is that they fail to challenge modern capitalism and its evils. In the United States they have actually functioned to maintain the status quo by persuading the electorate that protecting the environment is the Number One moral and political issue. This is what Richard Neuhaus has aptly termed 'the seduction of radicalism'; attention has been diverted from the poor and oppressed, and from the pursuit of justice for them which should always be the political priority of a nation. What point does the Harlem mother of six who is denied welfare see in preserving the Alaska wilderness for posterity? I say this as someone who, God knows, loves mountains and wild places, but when it comes to listing moral and political priorities I do not see how I can make my personal penchant for hillwalking into something sacred and place it above the needs of the poor and oppressed. If you want to place me on a political map, then mine is a left wing rather than a right wing criticism of the environmental movement.

But this still does not tell us how to view the environment. The problems remain. How are Americans to restore the environment to its proper position as an essentially political issue, over which reasonable people will disagree? How can they end the holy war between preservationists and developers in which each side castigates the other as the devil incarnate? How can we regain the attitude of those earlier ages which saw the natural world as pointing to the divine without itself being divine? How can we cherish our environment without making a fetish of it?

Perhaps we need to recover that part of the biblical view of the material world which Protestants have traditionally neglected: that it is given us not only to use but also to *enjoy*. The Puritans understood that because there were no sacred spirits in the material world they were therefore freed to develop its resources. What I would like to emphasize is that, for the same reason, we are freed to enjoy it. Since there is no ultimate meaning in the tangible world, since it is not sacred, we are free to inject our own meanings into it and to enjoy it in the light of those meanings, without ever taking them too seriously, without ever making them absolute. Only when our search for the sacred is directed away from the world are we freed to enjoy the world. Perhaps only then will human beings feel at home in their environment without having to lie to themselves about it.

Notes

Chapter One   INTRODUCTION: AN ENCHANTED WORLD?

1. As will become apparent in the course of the book, I have two further disagreements with White: his negative evaluation of the disenchanting of the world, and his assertion that Christianity's view of nature is man-centred.

Chapter Two   THE RELIGION OF NATURE

1. Robin Clarke, *Notes for the Future*, Thames and Hudson, 1975, p. 11.
2. Thomas Kuhn, *The Structure of Scientific Revolutions*, University of Chicago Press, 1962.
3. D. Owen, *What is Ecology?*, Oxford University Press, 1974, pp. v–vi.
4. V. Ferkiss, *The Future of Technological Civilization*, Braziller, 1974, chapters 8 and 9.
5. K. A. Erickson, 'Ceremonial Landscapes of the American West' in *Landscape*, 22, 1977, pp. 39–47. See also G. Seddon, 'The Rhetoric and Ethics of the Environmental Protest Movement' in *Meanjin Quarterly*, 31, pp. 427–438.
6. Michael Allaby, *Inventing the Future*, Hodder, 1976, p. 71.
7. T. O'Riordan, *Environmentalism*, Pion, 1976, p. 11.
8. Mircea Eliade, *The Sacred and the Profane*, Harper & Row, 1959.
9. Mircea Eliade, *The Sacred and the Profane*, pp. 118–125; Edwyn Bevan, *Symbolism and Belief*, Allen & Unwin, 1938, p. 61ff.
10. Edward Abbey, *Desert Solitaire*, Ballantine, 1971, p. 60.
11. K. A. Erickson, pp. 39–47.
12. David Brower (ed), *Wildlands in our Civilization*, Sierra Club, 1964, pp. 14, 61, 49.
13. Robert Marshall, 'The Problem of the Wilderness' in *Scientific Monthly*, 30, 1930, pp. 141–148.
14. See Leo Marx, *The Machine in the Garden*, Oxford University Press, 1964.
15. Roderick Nash, *Wilderness and the American Mind*, Yale University Press, 1973, p. 67.
16. David Lowenthal, 'The Place of the Past in the American Landscape', chapter 4 in D. Lowenthal & M. J. Boyden (eds), *Geographies of the Mind*, Oxford University Press, 1976.

17. Anthony Smith, *Wilderness*, Allen & Unwin, 1978, p. 17.
18. G. H. Haines, *Whose Countryside?*, Dent, 1973, p. 79.
19. This has been aptly caricatured by Horace Miner, 'Body Ritual among the Nacirema' in *American Anthropologist*, 58, 1956, pp. 503–507.
20. C. S. Lewis, *Miracles*, Bles, 1947, p. 33.

Chapter Three   THE SANCTITY OF THE INDIVIDUAL

1. John Berger, *Ways of Seeing*, Penguin, 1972, p. 16.
2. *Ibid*, pp. 48–49.
3. Christopher Tunnard, *A World with a View: an inquiry into the nature of scenic values*, Yale University Press, 1978, p. 57.
4. R. Neuhaus, *In Defense of People*, Macmillan, 1970, p. 146.
5. Basil Bernstein, *Class, Codes and Control*, Routledge, 1971, p. 184; Mary Douglas, *Natural Symbols*, Barrie & Jenkins, 1973, pp. 190–191.
6. J. A. Walter, *A Long Way From Home*, Paternoster, 1979, chapters 3 and 4; also my forthcoming book on the wilderness.
7. Lewis Mumford, *The City in History*, Penguin, 1966, pp. 310–11.
8. See Anton Zijderveld, *The Abstract Society*, Allen Lane, 1972, pp. 13–15.
9. Margaret Drabble, *A Writer's Britain*, Thames & Hudson, 1979, p. 8.
10. T. O'Riordan, *Environmentalism*, Pion, 1976, p. 314.
11. The fact that society actually encourages us to surround ourselves with such 'unique' ethnic objects merely highlights how assiduous people have to be in their distancing. For an entertaining discussion of the endless complexities, see Stanley Cohen & Laurie Taylor, *Escape Attempts: the theory and practice of resistance to everyday life*, Allen Lane, 1976.
12. Mircea Eliade, *The Sacred and the Profane*, Harper & Row, 1959, p. 29.

Chapter Four   SACRED AND PROFANE IN LANDSCAPE: HISTORICAL ORIGINS

1. This concept of leisure applies only to those in paid employment and to schoolchildren. Housewives do not have clearly marked blocks of time called 'leisure', though they may be incorporated into some of the activities with which their husbands fill their leisure, for example the Sunday afternoon family drive in the country.

2. Where this trend leaves the housewife who has no leisure (see note 1) is a serious and much under-discussed question which cannot be explored here.

3. Harold Osborne, *Aesthetics and Art Theory*, Longman, 1968, p. 99.

4. Accepted, that is, by townspeople. Farmers and their workers still find beauty in a well-ploughed field or a well-drained meadow.

Chapter Five   SACRED AND PROFANE IN LANDSCAPE: CONTEMPORARY PROBLEMS

1. Harold Osborne, *Aesthetics and Art Theory*, Longman, 1968, p. 103.

2. Emile Durkheim, *The Elementary Forms of the Religious Life*, Allen & Unwin, 1976, pp. 40–41.

3. L. Allison, *Environmental Planning*, Allen & Unwin, 1975.

4. Roger Pilkington's foreword to Frederic Doerflinger's book *Slow Boat Through England*, Allan Wingate, 1970.

5. Margaret Drabble, *A Writer's Britain*, Thames & Hudson, 1979, p. 218.

6. This is reprinted in Ken Wilson (ed), *The Games Climbers Play*, Diadem Books, 1978.

Chapter Six   THE ENVIRONMENT AS SAVIOUR

1. Quoted in D. W. Meinig (ed), *The Interpretation of Ordinary Landscapes*, Oxford University Press, 1979, p. 135.

2. Henry Nash Smith, *Virgin Land: the American West as symbol and myth*, Harvard University Press, 1950, chapter 20.

3. Frederick Jackson Turner, *The Frontier in American History*, Henry Holt, 1920.

4. James E. Vance, Jr., 'California and the Search for the Ideal' in *Annals of the Association of American Geographers*, Vol. 62, No. 2, 1972, pp. 185–210.

5. J. B. Jackson, 'The Order of a Landscape', in Meinig, *op. cit.*

6. As argued by Lynn White Jr., 'The Historical Roots of our Ecologic Crisis' in *Science*, March 1967.

7. See W. R. Burch, *Daydreams and Nightmares*, Harper & Row, 1971.

Chapter Seven   HOUSEWIVES ALL

1. I am indebted for this example to Brian Farrington of the Language Laboratory, Aberdeen University.

2. In *Africa*, Vol. 37, 1967.
3. Karl Marx & Frederick Engels, *The German Ideology*, Lawrence & Wishart, 1965, p. 39.
4. Mircea Eliade, *Images and Symbols: studies in religious symbolism* Harvill Press, 1961, chapter 1.
5. Ann Oakley, *The Sociology of Housework*, Martin Robertson, 1974, pp. 104–5.
6. In D. L. Barker & S. Allen (eds), *Dependence and Exploitation in Work and Marriage*, Longman, 1976.

Chapter Eight   AT HOME WITH NATURE

1. Raymond Williams, *Keywords*, Fontana, 1976, p. 186.
2. I am indebted in what follows to an (as far as I am aware) unpublished lecture by the late Prof. Hans Rookmaaker on 'Nature and Grace in Late Medieval Art'.
3. Leo Marx, *The Machine in the Garden*, Oxford University Press, 1964, p. 197.
4. Quoted in P. J. Schmitt, *Back to Nature*, Oxford University Press, 1969, p. 175.

Chapter Nine   SIGHTSEEING

1. Sylvia Crowe, *Tomorrow's Landscape*, Architectural Press, 1963, p. 91.
2. Yi-Fu Tuan, *Topophilia*, Prentice Hall, 1974, p. 137.
3. Robin Collomb, *Alpine Points of View*, Neville Spearman, 1961, p. 229.
4. J. A. Walter, *A Long Way From Home*, Paternoster, 1979, chapter 8.
5. 'At Auschwitz, a discordant atmosphere of tourism' in *New York Times*, 3 November 1974.
6. Galen Rowell, *Many People Come, Looking, Looking*, Allen & Unwin, 1981.

Chapter Ten   SYMBOLS OF FREEDOM

1. Though see my forthcoming book on the wilderness, for a study of how even space may not always be devoid of human meaning.
2. The wilderness is a major symbol of freedom in the United States. See my forthcoming book.
3. Paul Corrigan, 'Out with the Lads' in *New Society*, No. 874, 5 July 1979, pp. 7–9.
4. Peter Marsh et al, *The Rules of Disorder*, Routledge, 1978.

5. Phil Cohen, 'Subcultural Conflict and Working Class Community' in *Working Papers in Cultural Studies* No. 2, Centre for Contemporary Cultural Studies, Birmingham University.
6. Paul Willis, *Learning to Labour*, Saxon House, 1977, p. 27.
7. Lewis Mumford, *The City in History*, Penguin, 1966, p. 586ff.
8. Jay Appleton, *The Experience of Landscape*, Wiley, 1975.

Chapter Eleven   ENVIRONMENTAL FEAR
1. I. Altman & J. F. Wohlwill (eds), *Children and the Environment*, Plenum Press, 1978, p. 102.
2. Stina Sandels, *Children in Traffic*, Elek, 1972, p. 1.
3. J. A. Walter, *Sent Away*, Saxon House, 1978, p. 106.
4. J. A. Walter, 'Bad Kids and Bad Homes' in *Faith and Thought*, Vol. 106, 1979, pp. 169–177.
5. D. Appleyard et al, *The View From the Road*, MIT Press, 1964, p. 10.
6. Ibid p. 13.
7. Robert Marshall, 'The Problem of the Wilderness' in *Scientific Monthly*, 30, 1930, p. 144.

Chapter Twelve   WHAT CAN WE DO WITH THE SPIRITS IN THE FOREST?
1. Quoted in D. Lowenthal, 'Past Time, Present Place' in *Geographical Review*, Vol. 65, No. 1, 1975, p. 13.
2. C. S. Lewis, *Miracles*, Bles, 1947, p. 89.
3. Leo Marx, 'Pastoral Ideals and City Troubles', chapter 7 in Ian G. Barbour (ed), *Western Man and Environmental Ethics*, Addison Wesley, 1973, pp. 111–2.
4. There are many different usages of the terms functionalism, rationalism, and materialism, which can be confusing. I trust my use of the terms is clear.
5. Anne Oakley, *The Sociology of Housework*, Martin Robertson, 1974, ch. 6. Another example of a study that tries to demystify the environment is my own forthcoming book on the wilderness.

Further reading

In the 'References' section, I have acknowledged the sources of quotations and passages where I have all but quoted an author. This appendix is for the reader who wants to follow up not detailed points, but the general ideas on which I have drawn. Where two dates of publication are given, the former (in brackets) refers to the date of first publication.

Chapter One   INTRODUCTION: AN ENCHANTED WORLD?

The article which stimulated the debate on the role of religion in our treatment of the environment is by Lynn White Jr, 'The Historical Roots of our Ecologic Crisis' in *Science*, Vol. 155, 10 March 1967, pp. 1203–7. This article and some of the subsequent debate may be found in Ian G. Barbour (ed), *Western Man and Environmental Ethics*, Addison-Wesley, 1973. Also important is Harvey Cox's *The Secular City*, Macmillan/SCM, 1965.

Chapter Two   THE RELIGION OF NATURE

Chapter 11 of Kenneth Clark's *Civilisation*, BBC Publications, 1969, provides a good introduction to the romantic worship of nature in the eighteenth and nineteenth centuries. A more general introduction to the philosophical ideas of the Enlightenment is Paul Hazard's *European Thought in the Eighteenth Century* (1946) Penguin, 1965.

An elaboration of my critique of political ecology may be found in chapter six of my book *A Long Way From Home*, Paternoster, 1979, and a more substantial critique from a Christian stance is Richard Neuhaus' *In Defense of People – ecology and the seduction of radicalism*, Macmillan, 1970. An excellent article by a Marxist is by Hans-Magnus Enzensberger, 'A Critique of Political Ecology' in *New Left Review*, No. 84, 1974.

A comprehensive history of the wilderness cult in America is Roderick Nash's *Wilderness and the American Mind*, (1967) Yale University Press, 1973, while Linda H. Graber, a student of Yi-Fu Tuan, examines the religious motifs in the wilderness cult in her book *Wilderness as Sacred Space*, Association of American Geographers, 1976.

The classic on the English landscape is W. G. Hoskins' *The Making of the English Landscape* (1955) Penguin, 1970, which cannot be recommended too highly. A sober sociological analysis of contemporary rural life is Howard Newby's *Green and Pleasant Land?*, Hutchinson, 1979. Newby also has an appropriately cutting review of the late 1970's fad for coffee table books on the countryside in *New Society*, 14 August 1980, pp. 324–5.

Any consideration of 'nature' should also take note of Mary Douglas' anthropological insights in *Natural Symbols*, Penguin, 1970.

Chapter Three   THE SANCTITY OF THE INDIVIDUAL
For further discussion of the twin idolatries of individualism and collectivism, and how they feed off each other, see my book *A Long Way From Home*, chapter 5.

In *The Invisible Religion*, Macmillan, 1967, leading sociologist Thomas Luckmann analyses the modern worship of the self. On the alienation from society felt by the modern individual, see Anton Zijderveld's work *The Abstract Society* (1970) Allen Lane, 1972.

John Berger, in his *Ways of Seeing*, Penguin, 1972, gives a stimulating introduction to several aspects of western art, such as perspective and possessiveness. Margaret Drabble's book *A Writer's Britain: Landscape in Literature*, Thames & Hudson, 1979, is a most readable illustrated study of how writers have expressed themselves, their ideas and their characters through written images of landscape; several of the literary quotations I have used are found in her book. See also the collection edited by D. C. D. Pocock, *Humanistic Geography and Literature*, Croom Helm/Barnes and Noble, 1981.

There are two comprehensive reviews of research done by

experimental psychologists on privacy, crowding, personal space and territoriality: they are I. Altman's *The Environment and Social Behaviour*, California: Brooks Cole, 1975, and P. M. Insel & H. C. Lindgren's *Too Close for Comfort: the psychology of crowding*, Prentice Hall, 1978.

Chapter Four SACRED AND PROFANE IN LANDSCAPE: HISTORICAL ORIGINS

A fascinating case study of an early nineteenth-century paternalist landowner/industrialist is Graham Mee's *Aristocratic Enterprise*, Blackie, 1975. Leo Marx's *The Machine in the Garden: technology and the pastoral ideal in America*, Oxford University Press, 1964, examines the tension between technology and the pastoral vision of America, drawing largely on literature, while Francis D. Klingender discusses how British painters treated early industry in *Art and the Industrial Revolution* (1947) Paladin, 1972.

E. F. Schumacher has several insights into the curious differences in values which govern the realms of production and consumption in *Small is Beautiful*, Abacus, 1973. On the development of these categories and of the Victorian notion of domesticity in which the woman's place is firmly in the home, see Leonore Davidoff's article 'The Rationalization of Housework' in D. L. Barker & S. Allen (eds), *Dependence and Exploitation in Work and Marriage*, Longman, 1976, and Catherine Hall's 'The Early Formation of Victorian Domestic Ideology' in Sandra Burman (ed), *Fit Work for Women*, Croom Helm, 1979.

On the difference between boys' and girls' experience of space: Erik Erikson's 'Inner and Outer Space: reflections of womanhood' in R. J. Lifton (ed), *The Woman in America*, Houghton Mifflin, 1965, gives a psychoanalytic interpretation; and R. Moore & D. Young's 'Childhood Outdoors' in I. Altman & J. F. Wohlwill (eds), *Children and the Environment*, Plenum Press, 1978, gives a review of experiments on the subject by environmental psychologists. The collection by Altman & Wohlwill is a useful way of getting into the literature on children's perception and use of their environment.

The classic text on the way the nouveaux riches need to display their new found wealth is Thorstein Veblen's *The Theory of the Leisure Class* (1899) Mentor Books, 1953.

Raymond Williams' *The Country and the City*, Chatto & Windus, 1973, is a brilliant study of the dichotomy between city and country as presented in English literature.

Chapter Five SACRED AND PROFANE IN LANDSCAPE: CONTEMPORARY PROBLEMS

On pollution, see Mary Douglas' *Purity and Danger*, Penguin, 1970. René Dubos argues that it is important that we care for the landscape of cities and that we do not channel all our ecological energies into preserving the wilderness: 'A Theology of the Earth', chapter 4 in Ian G. Barbour's *Western Man and Environmental Ethics*. In *The Unofficial Countryside*, Collins, 1973, Richard Mabey celebrates the wildlife to be found in grimiest London: a spirited attack on the prevalent notion that beauty is only found miles away in national parks and the like.

Chapter Six THE ENVIRONMENT AS SAVIOUR

The worldview typically held by traditional societies is described by Mircea Eliade in several books, but in this chapter I have drawn particularly on his book *The Myth of the Eternal Return* (1949) Princeton University Press, 1954, which was re-published in 1959 under the title *Cosmos and History*, Harper Torchbooks. Confirmation of Eliade's contention that the African has no concept of the future may be found in an article by John S. Mbiti, 'The African Concept of Time' in *Africa*, Vol 8, 1967. For a general survey of different notions of history, see David Bebbington's *Patterns in History* Inter-Varsity Press, 1979.

For a stimulating study of the hope that Americans have placed in their land, see a book by William R. Burch, Jr., *Daydreams and Nightmares: a sociological essay on the American environment*, Harper & Row, 1971. Robert Hughes'

The Shock of the New, BBC Publications, 1980, contains a chapter on the modern movement in architecture which reveals the utopian faith behind it.

The tendency to romanticize the past is discussed critically in the two works by Howard Newby mentioned earlier. An erudite geographer's view is David Lowenthal's article 'Past Time, Present Place: landscape and memory' in *Geographical Review*, Vol. 65, No. 1, 1975, pp. 1–36, while in his book *What Time is this Place?*, MIT Press, 1972, Kevin Lynch tries to lay a basis for the use of the past by town planners.

Chapter Seven   HOUSEWIVES ALL

On homelessness as the basic human condition, see Peter Berger's *Invitation to Sociology* (1963) Penguin, 1966, and Peter Berger, Brigitte Berger & Hansfried Kellner's *The Homeless Mind*, (1973) Penguin, 1974, for a sociological approach. For a theological approach to the same question, see the writings of Jacques Ellul, in particular *The Meaning of the City*, Eerdmans, 1970 and *The New Demons*, Mowbrays, 1976. For an attempt to integrate the theological and sociological approaches, see my book *A Long Way From Home*.

The approach to landscape which sees it as an expression of culture is a theme running through much of the work of the anthropologist Mary Douglas, and is central to the highly original articles on the American landscape by J. B. Jackson, founder and editor until the late 1960s of the journal *Landscape*; some of Jackson's essays are brought together in *The Necessity for Ruins, and other Topics*, University of Massachusetts Press, 1980. Cultural or 'humanistic' geography also tends to take this approach; see in particular Yi-Fu Tuan's *Topophilia*, Prentice Hall, 1974; David Lowenthal & Martyn J. Boyden (eds) *Geographies of the Mind*, Oxford University Press, 1976; and D. W. Meinig (ed) *The Interpretation of Ordinary Landscapes*, Oxford University Press, 1979.

For a completely different approach to landscape, based on the model of man the hunter, see Jay Appleton's *The

Experience of Landscape, Wiley, 1975.

On the symbolic aspects of the private house, see Amos Rapoport's *House Form and Culture*, Prentice Hall, 1969; this has many useful snippets of information, but does not hang together well as a book, possibly because the author has no coherent theory from which to interpret his facts.

On housework, by far and away the most revealing writing is by Ann Oakley, in particular *Housewife* (1974) Penguin, 1976. *The Sociology of Housework*, Martin Robertson, 1974, adds little other than a lot of needless sociological jargon, though chapter 6 'Routines and Standards' is definitely worth reading.

Chapter Eight   AT HOME WITH NATURE
On the Hebrew view of land, see Walter Brueggemann's *The Land*, SPCK, 1977. Any consideration of western concepts of nature could do a lot worse than start with the few pages on 'nature' in Raymond Williams' *Keywords*, Fontana, 1976. On possessiveness in art, see John Berger's *Ways of Seeing*. Lynn White, Jr, considers that medieval theology was man-centred, not God-centred as I claim; he puts this view in 'Continuing the Conversation', chapter 5 in Ian G. Barbour's *Western Man and Environmental Ethics*.

For a popular critique by a Christian of the view that the scientific picture of man is the only one, see Donald M. MacKay's *The Clockwork Image*, Inter-Varsity Press, 1974. H. Paul Santmire has examined how romanticism and scientism can co-exist in the same person, and concludes that both represent an attempt to escape from the insecurities of history: 'Historical Dimensions of the American Crisis', chapter 6 in Ian G. Barbour's *Western Man and Environmental Ethics*.

Chapter Nine   SIGHTSEEING
Susan Sontag's book *On Photography*, Allen Lane, 1977, is very stimulating. Dean Maccannell's *The Tourist*, Macmillan, 1976, makes the tourist out to be a model of modern man; an interesting thesis, not incompatible with mine, though hard

going in places. Erik Cohen's article 'A Phenomenology of Tourist Experiences' in *Sociology*, Vol. 13, No. 2, May 1979, pp. 179–201, points out that there are several types of tourist; despite its title, it is quite easy going.

On pilgrimage, see Victor & Edith Turner's *Image and Pilgrimage in Christian Culture: anthropological perspectives*, Blackwell, 1978.

Chapter Ten   SYMBOLS OF FREEDOM

On space and place, see F. W. Dillistone's *Traditional Symbols and the Contemporary World*, Epworth, 1973, for the theological implications; and Yi-Fu Tuan's *Space and Place*, Edward Arnold, 1977, for the geographical implications.

Lewis Mumford, in his encyclopaedic *The City in History* (1961) Penguin, 1966, is impressed more with the vibrancy of the social and political life of a city than with the grandness of its architecture, and shows how the two rarely go together; human fraternity rather than totalitarian order is the standard by which Mumford judges cities. For a very positive view of the potential disorder of city life, see Richard Sennett's *The Uses of Disorder*, Allen Lane, 1971.

On the American penchant for moving, or rather for creating myths about those who are constantly on the move, see David E. Sopher's article 'The Landscape of Home' in D. W. Meinig (ed) *The Interpretation of Ordinary Landscapes*.

Chapter Eleven   ENVIRONMENTAL FEAR

Paul Tillich's book *The Courage To Be*, Nisbet, 1952, is difficult and perhaps a little dated philosophically, but it is essential reading for anyone exploring human anxiety. Yi-Fu Tuan's *Landscapes of Fear*, Blackwell, 1980, is a veritable mine of insight and information.

The difficulty with which children cope with traffic is alarmingly, though prosaicly, presented by Stina Sandels in *Children in Traffic* (1968) Paul Elek, 1972. Philippe Aries' work *Centuries of Childhood*, Cape, 1962, is a classic on the historical origins of our present high evaluation of childhood.

A lovely little article on how ill people experience their

bodies is Eric J. Cassell's 'Disease as an "It" ' in *Social Science & Medicine*, Vol. 10, 1976, pp. 143–6.

Oscar Newman, in his *Defensible Space*, Architectural Press, 1976, describes how, with the aid of good design, residents of high-rise apartments may regain control of the precincts of their homes. Celia Fremlin's important exposé of how fear rather than reality is what makes women stay at home at night is 'Walking in London at Night' in *New Society*, 19 April, 1979, pp. 132–4.

On the taboo on talking about death, see Geoffrey Gorer's *Death, Grief and Mourning in Contemporary Britain*, Cresset Press, 1965, and Philippe Aries' *Western Attitudes Toward Death: from the Middle Ages to the present*, Johns Hopkins University Press, 1974.

Chapter Twelve   WHAT CAN WE DO WITH THE SPIRITS IN THE FOREST?

Attempts to arrive at, or at least describe, spiritual truth from the starting point of the everyday world are made by Michel Quoist in his *Prayers of Life* (1954) Gill, 1963, and by Peter Berger in his *A Rumour of Angels*, Penguin, 1970, chapter 3.

Monotheism's aversion to seeking the sacred within the human and material world is clearly stated in Jacques Ellul's *The New Demons* and my own *A Long Way From Home*. A Christian celebration of the material beauty of the world is Calvin Seerveld's *Rainbows for the Fallen World*, Tuppence Press, 1980. I take my views on the importance of enjoyment and truth further in an article on mountaineering, 'To Know is to Love' in *Mountain*, No. 78, March/April 1981, pp. 46–7. For the debate on the responsibility of Christianity for our present ecological mess, see Ian G. Barbour's *Western Man and Environmental Ethics*.

Functionalism and rationalism are so ingrained in our modern way of thinking that one could hardly single out any one work as more representative than any other.

Index